30 g droždí
500 g polohrubé ...
80 g cukru
70 g másla
2 žloutky
300 ml mléka
500 g čerstvých švestek, meruně...
Drobenka
110 g hladké mouky
30 g cukru
70 g másla

Předehřát troubu na 180°, vy ma...
zamíchejte cukr, mouku a drožd...
mě promíchejte. Zahřejte mléko na...
rozpusťte v něm máslo a zamých...

Stories & Supper - more than a recipe book is supported by Waltham Forest London Borough of Culture 2019

Headline Partners

M walthamstow   Uber Eats   Homes for rent by at BLACKHORSE MILLS   Taylor Wimpey

Official Funding Partners

LOTTERY FUNDED   ARTS COUNCIL ENGLAND   HERITAGE FUND   Paul Hamlyn Foundation

A Mayor of London initiative supported by

MAYOR OF LONDON   London   airbnb

Winning Borough

Waltham Forest

Stories & Supper

more than a recipe book

Editor: Helen Taylor

Assistant Editors: Olivia Sheringham and Julie Yip

Graphic design: Angela Lyons

Cover illustration: Sophie Herxheimer

Food photography: John Nassari

Food styling: Oliver Rowe and Sanchia Lovell

Portrait photography: Laura Martinez (Abdullah, Laura, Mary, Mohamed Alie and Shahnaz); John Nassari (Gee and Kahraman); Luke Natoli (Suleiman); Lucy B for Leytonstone Loves Film 2019 (Maurice)

Additional photography: Simon Goodwin (pages 17 bottom left, 58, 69 top left, 93 top); Camilla Greenwell (pages 9, 17 middle right, 36 bottom right, 128); Deniz Huseyin (page 33, 36 bottom left); Jimmy Lee (page 93 middle right); Laura Martinez (pages 26, 99 bottom, 114, 139); David Monteith-Hodge (page 102); John Nassari (pages 6, 93 top, middle left and bottom right); Luke Natoli (pages 10, 17 top, middle left and bottom right, 47 bottom, 69 top right and bottom, 134); James Robertshaw (pages 16, 46, 47 top, 92, 119); Helen Taylor (pages 36 top left, top right, middle right, 68, 83, 93 bottom left, 98, 99 top and middle); Trinity College London (page 107)

Additional text: Shalinee Basak, Filiz Emre Cooke, Jane Longshaw, Douglas Saltmarshe, Freddie Seelig

Proofreading: Deniz Huseyin

First published in Great Britain by Stories & Supper in 2019
www.storiesandsupper.co.uk

© Stories & Supper 2019

Printed and bound in Wales by Gomer Press, Llandysul Enterprise Park, Llandysul, Ceredigion SA44 4JL

ISBN: 978-1-5272-5079-6

Contents

Stories & Supper

Stories & Supper was founded in East London in early 2017, when the words 'migrant crisis' were on every TV screen and newspaper front page, but the real stories of those making the difficult decision to leave their homes were hard to find. Our founder Rebecca Tully had a hunch that if the people who were making the journeys were able to share their stories on their own terms, in a welcoming and safe environment, then it would start to challenge some of the assumptions about migration.

But we needed to find people prepared to listen.

We knew that food was a way to bring people together, so we embraced the growing appetite for exciting global cuisine and launched our supper club project. This meant that as well as creating a space where stories could be shared, we were able to offer refugee and migrant chefs the chance to showcase their skills. Since then, we've served hundreds of supper guests outstanding food from countries including Sudan, India, Syria, Iran, Burma, Bangladesh and Afghanistan.

While our supper guests have enjoyed food from around the world, they have listened to stories about why people feel compelled to leave their homes, about difficult journeys and the labyrinthine nature of the UK asylum system. But we have also been committed to presenting stories which shatter assumptions about the kind of people who become burdened with the label 'refugee' or 'migrant'. There has been poetry, music and comedy, alongside informal conversations, rehearsed speeches and impromptu contributions.

Keen to reach a wider audience, we started to branch out beyond supper clubs and run different kinds of events. We held 'street food and storytelling' pop-ups at the Walthamstow Garden Party, hosted a screening and panel discussion at the first Leytonstone Loves Film festival, and ran a story café project in collaboration with Queen Mary University, sharing migration stories with colleges and community centres.

At the heart of everything we do is our team – a community made up of refugees, recent and long-term migrants, and local volunteers. We meet weekly to share stories, test recipes, plan events and have fun. Whatever we are doing we always eat together. We know how important food is for nourishing the body and the soul. Cooking and eating with each other creates bonds and breaks down barriers, and the friendships we have formed as a result transcend cultural and linguistic differences.

The time, energy, love and commitment that everyone involved in Stories & Supper has given to the project over the past few years speaks volumes. It is a fitting riposte to all those who say that we cannot live together, who argue that our differences are insurmountable, that migration is out of control and is changing the fabric of our society.

This book represents our latest venture. With support from Waltham Forest London Borough of Culture 2019, we have been able to capture some of the recipes and stories we have shared so they can have a life beyond our events. Waltham Forest, where we are based, is a diverse and vibrant part of London with a long history of migration and welcome. We are proud to be part of that ongoing history.

Introduction

The recipes in this book remind their authors of home, of family and friends near or far. They conjure up memories of childhood, of beloved grandparents, special feasts and comforting everyday meals. They are twists on old favourites, a testament to how food evolves over time in new circumstances. They are cherished family recipes, passed down through generations – and now shared with you.

Some of the recipes have been cooked at our events, like Shahnaz's paneer curry (page 60) – once tasted never forgotten, or Hawari's Aswad salad (page 38) – a Sudanese version of aubergine dip. We have classic dishes from West Africa – Mary's Fufu with Peanut Soup from Ghana (page 88), Maurice's Ofe Egusi from Nigeria (page 94) and Mohamed Alie's Cassava Leaf Stew from Sierra Leone (page 96). We have also included recipes from our volunteers, many of whom have their own fascinating migration stories. Eva from the Czech Republic and Inbar from Israel contributed two delicious yeasted cakes (pages 116 and 118), demonstrating the journeys made by the Jewish diaspora and their cuisine.

For those who have been forced to leave their home country, arrival in the UK can produce a mixture of emotions. The sense of relief at having reached safety can be dampened by the long and tortuous asylum process. Living on £5 a day without permission to work, while in precarious shared accommodation, can seem like the very opposite of a warm welcome. In such circumstances, there is often a yearning for the tastes of home to make unfamiliar surroundings feel more familiar.

Sometimes, it takes a phone call back home to learn how to recreate a favourite dish. Abdullah spoke to his mum to find out the secrets of Nokaw (page 78) – a delicious Kurdish lamb and chickpea stew. He burned it at the first attempt, but has now perfected it and cooks it for all his friends. He also explained that cooking for one and eating alone is alien to people who have always eaten with extended family. We hope that the meals we share at Stories & Supper have, to some degree, recreated this sense of belonging.

The title of this book is *Stories & Supper: More Than a Recipe Book* and we hope it lives up to that promise. It is a recipe book, yes, but it is also a book filled with powerful and important stories. Stories that have been told at our events, or shared at our workshops.

They are stories of courage and determination, a testimony to the strength of the human spirit. But they are also difficult stories: Stories about the reasons why people leave behind everything that was familiar to them – their country, their jobs, their friends, their family. Stories about how people are treated when they seek asylum, about the indignity of detention centres, becoming homeless once Leave to Remain has been granted. Stories about a lack of understanding of the many reasons why women feel compelled to flee.

We think it is important that these stories are heard and make no apologies for including them in the book. But we have only included stories that the tellers are happy to share, other stories remain untold. The storytellers are the authors of their own lives – they are victims of circumstances beyond their control, but they are not victims per se. If you feel moved or inspired by their stories, we hope you also feel angry at the injustices within them. Maybe you will decide to campaign for refugee and migrants' rights, to volunteer or simply extend a hand of welcome.

The process of producing this book was as unorthodox as the book itself. We gathered stories and recipes during our story workshops, interviewing each other, writing fragments down on scraps of paper. We sent numerous WhatsApp messages seeking clarification, searching online for translations of ingredients, discovering new flavours along the way. And so the book's content emerged gradually out of these encounters.

We cooked recipes together and asked friends to test them too. We learned from each other about different ways of cooking and the range of ingredients used around the world, but were often surprised to discover the commonalities between different cuisines. Cassava in its various forms cropped up many times, the root pounded in fufu or eba and the leaves in Sierra Leonean stews. Lentils made their way into Bangladeshi fritters, Indian dals and Turkish soup. Various manifestations of cornmeal appeared in bread (page 130), as a coating for fish (page 18), or as the main ingredient in Venezuelan arepas (page 42). And vine leaves turn up in three versions of dolmas (we couldn't help ourselves) from Kurdistan, Turkey and Cyprus (pages 48-53).

The following people all contributed recipes, stories or ideas to make this book happen and it is a testament to their enthusiasm and commitment: Mary Attaa Adwoah, Suleiman Ali, Shalinee Basak, Shahnaz Begum, Susana Oduro Biamah, Filiz Emre Cooke, Kate Duffy, Goitom Fesshaye, Hawari Abdelaziz Hassan Mohamed, Jocelyn Hutchins, Mohamed Alie Jalloh, Abdullah Khalid, Yangla Lama, Jane Longshaw, Sanchia Lovell, Gee Manoharan, Laura Martinez, Jumana Moon, Syed Haleem Najibi, Maurice Nwokeji, Winnie Roach, Douglas Saltmarshe, Karel Schling, Freddie Seelig, Olivia Sheringham, Mariam Siddiqui, Tasnim and Noorjahan Sultanah, Inbar Tamari, Helen Taylor, Rebecca Tully, Eva Turner , Kahraman Yadirgi, Julie Yip and Tim Cheung Yip.

This book would also never have emerged in this form without the team of creatives who embraced our vision. Designer Angela Lyons, photographer John Nassari, and chefs and food stylists Oliver Rowe and Sanchia Lovell all worked their magic, while Sophie Herxheimer created a lovely cover illustration. We were also delighted that Stories & Supper member, photographer Laura Martinez, shot some beautiful portraits for us.

Food is never simply nourishment – it is an expression of love, a way of building community, a demonstration of hospitality, a way of remembering people and places. And this is more than a recipe book. It's a chance for us to share with you the connections we have made, the community we have built, the stories that have been told and the meals we have eaten.

We hope you enjoy cooking the recipes in your own home, and helping these important stories find new audiences, so that together we can write a different narrative about migration. **Helen Taylor**

BEGINNINGS

Pakora
Shahnaz – India

Ingredients

1 large bulb of garlic

1kg onions, peeled

15 green chillies

1 large bunch of fresh coriander

½tsp ground turmeric

2tbsp cumin seeds

2tbsp ajwain seeds

500g gram flour

1 litre vegetable oil (or enough for deep frying)

Makes about 30

Method

Separate and peel the garlic cloves. Blend the garlic to a paste, using a stick blender, adding a little water. Cut the onions in half and then slice into half moons. Chop the chillies, keeping the seeds if you want more heat. Wash and chop the coriander.

Mix the garlic, onions and chillies with the turmeric, cumin and ajwain in a large bowl. Add most of the gram flour. Adding a little cold water at a time, mix until the batter reaches a consistency that is neither too runny nor too dry – like thick yoghurt. Add more flour or water if needed. Mix well so all the ingredients are equally distributed.

Pour enough oil into a large pan or deep fat fryer for deep frying and heat until very hot, about 180°C. You will need room in the pan for the pakoras to cook without touching each other and without touching the bottom of the pan. Check the heat of the oil by dropping in a small piece of batter. If it sizzles right away, it's hot enough.

When the oil is ready, take a tablespoon sized amount of the mixture and gently place into the hot oil. Fry until golden brown. It's easier to drop the mixture into the oil using your hand, if you don't mind getting messy.

Repeat with the rest of the mixture, cooking in batches, taking care not to overcrowd the pan. Remove the pakora with a slotted spoon and place on a single layer on kitchen paper to drain and keep crispy until serving.

Serve with the mango chutney or tamarind chutney on page 135.

Pakora are sold as an evening snack in India in winter. And it's complusory to have them at Hindu vegetarian weddings!

They are usually served as a starter here and everybody loves them. You don't have to use onion – you can make them with spinach or many other vegetables.

Shahnaz – India

I come from South India. I was born in Nalgunda district and I grew up in Nagar Kurnool. My childhood, my education was there. I have many memories from there – I went to school there until my 'A' Levels. I had a happy childhood. After that I moved to the city, to Hyderabad, when I was 16. We built a house and the whole family moved there.

My mother cooked very nice food. Biryani, dal, aubergine curry and chicken. It was very tasty. She always cooked meat, not vegetarian. She made a soup called siri paye, made with goat's head and goat's legs. It's a bone soup. She cooked everything very nicely, but she wouldn't let me in the kitchen. All the time she told me to go and study.

India is a very big country. The food varies in different regions. In some places it is more spicy, in some more savoury. Hyderabadi biryani is very famous. Hindus love Muslim food, and we love their spicy food. Politics creates problems, but I always studied in mixed schools. We were always together. First comes humanity, then comes religion. And when I came to London, many good Hindu friends helped me too.

I got married at 20 to a Bangladeshi. I met him in Saudi Arabia where I was working. And after we married, I moved to Bangladesh where I lived with my husband's family. They had people working in their fields. They weren't paid, they just worked for lunch and dinner. Some of the ladies didn't even have blouses. In my culture, when you get married you are given a lot of clothes. So I used to give these ladies my clothes, my saris. I would give them rice secretly as well, and other food. I would hide the food in my sari. My mother-in-law didn't like to give to people outside the family.

My husband's whole family abused me and the marriage was violent. So I had to take my daughter and run. I went back to India, to my childhood home to make myself safe. Then my friends helped me come to the UK to try and settle my life. I wanted to give my daughter a good life. I did try to get some property in India, but my father refused me because of my divorce.

I came here to the UK in 2010 on a student visa, which lasted until 2014. After that I told immigration about my situation, about why I was here. I didn't know that I could seek asylum. I didn't know the meaning of asylum. Then one morning, at 5am, the immigration came to my house. I wasn't well at the time, I had vertigo. They were banging on the doors. I was in shock. It was September 2015 and they took me to Yarl's Wood detention centre for six days.

I was so stressed at that time, but there was a friend from college who was also here in the UK. He was like my family, like a brother, and I started cooking for him. I had to leave my daughter and family because of violence. But when I met this friend, he cheered me up. He made me laugh. He didn't know how to cook and he asked me to cook for him and share food together. With the stress in my life, I had stopped cooking. Then this friend encouraged me to cook for him and eat with him like a brother.

Then I went to the Refugee Council to ask for help and they referred me to the Red Cross in Dalston, East London. They serve lunch there and I noticed that people were throwing

the food away. This is haram [forbidden] in my religion. I first went there during Ramadan so I was fasting, I couldn't eat. But I was looking and asking, why are people throwing away food when it's free? When I finished fasting I ate a meal there and it had no taste at all!

After that I started cooking the food, adding flavour – ginger, garlic, cumin, curry powder, coriander leaves, a little bit of chilli. Then everyone started eating and there was no waste. I've been volunteering at the Red Cross for three years, cooking every Thursday. Everyone who comes to the Red Cross has stress, everyone has problems. They live in shelters and aren't able to cook. So I like to feed them. When they come there, they eat a home-cooked meal, sit around and chat. It makes them happy. And when I see them like that, I am happy.

I came to Stories & Supper in February 2017, when it first started, and I'm still here. Since I have been coming I have got more confidence. Everyone supports me and understands my problems. We tell stories and cook together. I've learned about food from other countries – Syria, Sudan, Iran. I've learned more skills, like talking in public, and I know how to feed 100 people now! I love to cook for events and I feel very pleased when I get feedback. It gives me more motivation. At the Walthamstow Garden Party, all the food we cooked was finished. That makes me very happy.

Now London is my home. Almost 10 years! Especially Waltham Forest. When I come out of the train in Leytonstone, I think, 'Thank God, I am home!' It is very multicultural. I was alone when I first came here, but this place has made me not feel lonely. I love it. I started a new life in 2017, with a new partner. He is Romanian and I am very happy with him.

Hamsi Kuşu (Anchovy Birds)
Filiz – Turkey

Ingredients

1kg fresh anchovies or small sardines
3 free-range eggs
100 to 150g fine cornmeal
Fine sea salt, to taste
200ml corn oil

Makes about 20, depending on size

Method

Ask your fishmonger to butterfly the anchovies or sardines, or butterfly them yourself (see instructions below). This removes all the bones and opens the fish out flat.

Mix the cornmeal with a little salt on a large flat plate. Beat the eggs lightly and place in a shallow bowl. Dip each fish first in the whisked egg and then in the cornflour, on both sides.

Heat the corn oil in a frying pan. When it is hot, fry the fish a few at a time until golden, making sure not to overcrowd the pan.

Serve with cornbread (see recipe on page 130) and a crisp salad.

To butterfly the fish:
Begin by removing the head and the guts, if not already removed. Then open out the fish and place it skin side up on a board. Hold the tail while you press firmly on the backbone with the back of your hand until the fish is flat. Turn the fish over and gently pull out the backbone, cutting it off when you reach the tail. Make sure that you remove any remaining small bones with a small knife or tweezers.

In Turkey, commercial fishing is forbidden in summer in order to maintain the stocks. So the fishing season – and the season for cooking and eating fish – begins when the ban is lifted at the start of September. My family on my father's side is originally from the Black Sea region of Turkey and they love anchovies and corn.

We love the fish season and as a family eat lots of fish in autumn, especially anchovies. We eat rice and anchovies, pan fried whole anchovies, or grilled anchovies. But my favourite is always these Anchovy Birds, especially when my babaanne (my paternal grandmother) cooks them.

They get their name because the fish resemble birds' wings when they are deboned and butterflied. When autumn comes, I always think of my grandmother and the delicious Anchovy Birds she used to make.

Piaju
Tasnim & Noorjahan – Bangladesh

THIS IS NOORJAHAN'S RECIPE FOR THESE LENTIL FRITTERS, WHICH WERE SERVED AS A STARTER AT ONE OF OUR SUPPER CLUBS

Ingredients

500g red split lentils

1 large onion, peeled

4 green chillies, or according to taste

2tbsp fresh coriander (optional)

Pinch of chilli flakes

1tsp cumin seeds

1 to 2tsp salt, or to taste

Oil for frying

Makes about 20 small fritters

Method

Soak the lentils overnight or for at least three hours. Drain the water half an hour before you are ready to cook.

Put the lentils in a food processor and blend until sticky, for about one minute. The grains should not be fine.

Finely chop the onion and chillies. De-seed the chillies if you want to limit the heat. Wash and chop the coriander, if using.

Put the lentils into a large mixing bowl and add all the other ingredients, except the oil. The mixture should not be too wet and should stick together when pressed.

Into a frying pan, add about 1cm of oil or enough for shallow frying.

Gently shape the lentil mixture into ping-pong sized balls and flatten gently so that the discs are about 1cm thick. You don't want them to be too thick or they won't cook properly.

Carefully place into the oil and cook on a medium heat. Fry the piaju until crispy and light golden brown. Turn over and cook the other side. Remove and place on kitchen paper to absorb excess oil.

Serve with chickpea salad or mint and coriander sauce.

Tasnim

My mum Noorjahan first came to the UK in 1982 with her husband, who moved to the UK to study and work. She has worked with various community groups in Waltham Forest, sharing her love of cooking along the way. This is the story of her first solo shopping trip:

"When I first came to the UK I knew very little English. The first place I lived was Amersham where there weren't many Asian people. One day my husband gave me some money to buy some vegetables. Back then in Bangladesh women rarely went grocery shopping, so this was a new experience for me. When I got to the shop I looked at the shopkeeper and said 'potato'. I couldn't form a full sentence. He looked confused and replied 'what?' Then I said 'cauliflower', but he still couldn't understand. I was determined to make this first trip a success, so I started to put vegetables in my basket. But the shopkeeper said: 'Ma'am this isn't self service.' I got scared and thought he would call the police. So I placed the £10 note my husband gave me on the counter, took the change and ran out with my shopping!"

Mercimek Çorbası (Lentil Soup)
Helen & Nesrin – Cyprus

Ingredients

75g broken rice (kırık pirinç)
250g red split lentils
1 large onion, peeled
1 carrot
2 large tomatoes
1tbsp sunflower or vegetable oil
2 litres of stock (vegetable or chicken)
Salt and pepper, to taste
1 lemon, to serve

Serves 6

Method

Soak the rice and lentils separately for two to three hours, or overnight if possible. This reduces the cooking time. Rinse and drain.

Peel the tomatoes by scoring them around the middle with a sharp knife, before plunging them into boiling water, then cold water. The skin should come off easily after this. Chop into small pieces.

Chop the onion finely and dice the carrot into 1cm cubes.

Pour the oil into a large saucepan and place on a low heat. Add the onion and carrot and fry gently for 15 minutes, to soften. Add the tomato and fry for a further 10 minutes.

Add the rice and lentils and stir to coat in the oil.

Carefully add half of the stock and place a lid on top, but not totally covering the pan.

Simmer gently for 30 minutes to an hour or more, depending on how long you soaked the rice and lentils. Add more stock or water as required.

Check to see that the rice and lentils are done and season with salt and pepper, to taste. You don't need to blend the soup, as it's meant to have some texture.

Serve with lemon wedges.

Helen

This recipe comes from my Turkish Cypriot mother-in-law Nesrin who came to the UK from Cyprus, via Australia, in the 1960s. It's the ultimate comfort food, simple yet totally satisfying. All Nesrin's children and grandchildren love it and it seems to have some kind of magical properties, as it's capable of lifting spirits, mending broken hearts and generally making the world seem like a better place.

Lentil soup is made across the Middle East, North Africa and the Mediterrean, but the Turkish Cypriots put broken rice in it, which makes it more substantial. A squeeze of lemon at the end is essential as it really lifts the flavour!

Tarka Dal
Shahnaz – India

Ingredients

10 cloves garlic, peeled
250g red lentils
1 green chilli
½tsp ground turmeric
Salt, to taste
1tsp ground cumin
2tsp ground coriander
1 tin chopped tomatoes
1 handful of fresh coriander,
plus extra to serve
Juice of 1 lemon

For the tarka

2tbsp sunflower oil
1tsp black mustard seeds
1tsp cumin seeds
2 dried red chillies

Serves 4

Method

To make the dal: First, chop the garlic, reserving three cloves for the tarka.

Wash the lentils and place them in a heavy bottomed saucepan. Add 1 litre of boiling water, the whole green chilli, 7 cloves of chopped garlic, the ground turmeric and a pinch of salt.

Bring to the boil and cook for about 15 minutes or until the lentils are almost cooked.

Add the cumin, ground coriander, tinned tomatoes, and half the fresh coriander and blend together using a hand blender. Simmer for 10-15 minutes. Taste and add more salt, if needed.

Add the lemon juice and cook for a further 5 minutes.

When the dal is almost ready, make the tarka: Heat the oil in a frying pan, add the rest of the chopped garlic, mustard seeds, cumin seeds and dried chillies. Cook for about 4 mins, until brown, but be careful not to burn.

Add the tarka to the dal. Sprinkle some fresh coriander on top, if liked.

Serve with basmati rice.

South Indians love dal. They would eat it for lunch or dinner – it's a very light food. You can eat it every day, with basmati rice and mango and lemon pickle, or tamarind pickle. Anyone who can afford lentils, can make dal.

You always need more lemons

We're lucky to have some great food shops near our base in Walthamstow, East London – as well as an amazing street market. No matter what ingredients we're looking for, we usually find them at one of the shops or stalls. Walthamstow High Street is like a living map of all the migrations that have occurred to the borough – Turkish supermarkets, Chinese grocery stores, Eastern European cafés, African fabric shops, Afghan suppliers. It's all here. Not forgetting the 'pound a bowl' market stalls, piled high with aubergines, chillies, ginger and garlic. And the most important thing we've learned on our many shopping trips? You always need more lemons than you think!

A couple of shops are our go-to places when we're shopping for our supper clubs or other events: International Supermarket, a Turkish shop selling fresh fruit and vegetables with an in-store bakery and a wide range of other goods, and Super Grows, a shop specialising in African and Asian vegetables, spices and dried food. Whatever's on our shopping list is usually in one of these two places. Gari? Tick. Aijwan seeds? Tick. Hibiscus flowers? Tick. Harina PAN maize flour? Tick. Fresh pomegranates? Tick. We chatted to both shops to find out what it's like serving the local area...

International Supermarket
International has been open for about 25 years. The original owners are Kurds who came to the UK as refugees from Turkey. When they got their residence permits they started a business, opening a small shop before buying other shops in nearby Leyton and Woodford. "Because they did a good job, had a good business, it grew in time," the current manager told us.

The new manager of International came to in the UK in 2003, after marrying his British-born Turkish wife, whose parents also came to the UK as refugees.

But International's customers aren't just Turkish: "There are people of every group; those of Turkish origin, Arabic origin, Pakistanis, all nationalities, a real mix. Europeans too. And because the customer profile is not fixed, it changes, we have to make sure we have a wide range of products in stock. From vegetables and fruit to meat, bread and simit. Everything is baked and sold fresh every day."

Super Grows
Nasir has been the owner and manager of Super Grows for nine years. The shop sells a wide range of products, including fresh herbs, spices, condiments, vegetables and dried and tinned produce. Over the years, product lines have been expanded to meet customer requests. The shop keeps a close eye on the quality and prices of local competition.

There are market stalls directly outside the shop and all the way down the longest outdoor market in Europe, as well as many other speciality shops selling international produce. Super Grows aims to attract custom by having the lowest prices. Customers who buy from the shop come from very many countries across the world. They are always alert to customer feedback, because being sensitive to their needs and keeping prices low makes for a successful business.

There are generally about six people working in the shop, keeping shelves stocked and serving customers. The staff come from India, Pakistan, Afghanistan, the West Indies and Somalia.

"Trade in Walthamstow has improved year on year," Nasir told us. "We have been successful. It has been a really good place to set up this type of business."

Pickled Aubergines
Inbar – Israel

Ingredients

3 aubergines

150ml olive or vegetable oil

1 bunch fresh coriander

5 cloves of garlic, peeled

3 fresh chillies or 1tsp dried chilli flakes

3 lemons, or to taste

Coarse sea salt, to taste

Method

Preheat the oven to 200°C/180°C Fan/Gas 6.

Top and tail the aubergines and slice into thin rounds.

Pour some of the oil into a baking tray and coat both sides of each slice of aubergine in the oil before placing in the tray. Keep the slices in a single layer, otherwise they won't cook properly. Add more oil if necessary and use more than one tray if you need to.

Place the aubergine in the oven for 20 minutes, checking after 15 minutes to make sure that they are not cooking too fast.

Meanwhile, wash the coriander. Then finely chop the garlic, fresh chilli (if using) and coriander. Mix together, adding the chilli flakes now (if using).

Juice the lemons and top up the juice with an equal amount of cold water. If your lemons are particularly large you may not want to use all the juice.

Once the aubergine slices are softened, golden in places and cooked through, remove from the oven.

In a large bowl or dish, layer about a quarter of the aubergine slices, then scatter over about a quarter of the chilli, garlic and coriander. Add salt to taste. Repeat the layers until all the aubergine is used up.

Pour over the lemon juice and water. Place a plate on top of the aubergine and weigh it down with something heavy. Leave for about one hour. Then remove the weights and the plate.

The aubergines are best enjoyed a day or two after they have been made and will keep for up to one week in the fridge.

They are delicious served with tahini dressing (see page 135), as part of a mezze or as a side dish with pretty much anything.

There is a famous Arab proverb that aubergine is meat without bones. You can cook it in so many different ways – fried or baked in the oven, or cooked whole to make baba ganoush. When I was a teenager I became a vegetarian – but I was a really weird vegetarian who didn't eat many vegetables! My mum kept trying to cook me things, but I didn't like them.

Then I went to summer camp and tried aubergine in a salad and loved it. So my mum tried lots of different ways with aubergines and this is one of the recipes I learned from her. It is normally made with vinegar, but one Passover night my grandfather decided that maybe it wasn't Kosher to have vinegar, so my mum tried it with lemons. The aubergines are traditionally fried, but I cook them in the oven because it's less work and is also healthier.

Gee – Sri Lanka

Spoiler alert! This is my story: I was detained when I was 21 years old in 2013, but was then released. And here I am with refugee status, simply feeling lucky and proud. But that's not the story I am going to tell here. I want to take you on a journey that I took four years ago. It was an improbable journey, from London to Belfast.

When I began to write my story, I was looking for inspiration. I was watching the TV series *Victoria* and, in one episode, Prince Albert said to Queen Victoria "Charity begins at home!" It's a simple sentence, but what does it even mean? Who does it apply to and who does it not apply to? Do I even agree with that sentence?

And then, looking for more inspiration, I started listening to Ed Sheeran. (No need to laugh – we've all done it at some point.) I stumbled upon his song *Castle on the Hill*. It was a song about the feeling of going home or the memories of being at home. Well, Ed Sheeran's experience of home is very different to mine.

As a Tamil speaking person, growing up in the East of Sri Lanka meant that I had to continuously look over my shoulder. There was always a question at night before bed: Will I make it to tomorrow?

Sri Lanka topped the *Lonely Planet's* number one destination to visit for 2019. Without doubt, it's a beautiful country. In contrast, Freedom from Torture (an organisation which advocates for survivors of torture) listed Sri Lanka as top of their list of countries producing torture survivors – for the last seven years.

While Ed Sheeran was running into an alleyway to get a sneaky kiss or smoke or drink, I was running to hide in a bunker from barrel bombs, falling from aircrafts.

I want you all to think about the last time you felt like going home. It might have been for your parent's birthday, or for Christmas. Most of you will feel very happy when you go home. Some of you will feel petrified at the prospect of having every single member of your family in one place for more than two days.

But some of us are terrified of going home, because there is no home. We are running away from it.

My journey began in Belfast on a normal day. The weather was dark and dull, as usual. As I was seeking asylum, I had to sign every week in a Home Office reporting centre. After the usual procedure, the reception staff told me to wait as they wanted to discuss my case. I waited and that was when the big shock came: A man in a black uniform armed with handcuffs and pepper spray. The uniform had a very close resemblance to that of Sri Lanka's death squad.

At the time I was convinced that the man had a gun. But thinking about it now, I can see that my sense of reality had begun to collapse. A deep fear made me accept everything he   >

said and I signed everywhere he wanted. I remember feeling like I was frozen, unable to move my limbs from the chair that I was sitting in.

After three hours of conversation and frequent begging, he allowed me to go back to my accommodation to pack my belongings. He handcuffed me and led me to my room, while my fellow housemates watched in distress. Then he gave me three minutes to pack my bags. I went crazy! I threw everything I could into one bag.

When I finally arrived at the detention centre, I went through my belongings and found that day's newspaper, olive oil, salt, a bedsheet and a half-eaten banana. I had left my valuables behind – my school certificates, money, gifts from my sisters, old photos, diaries and a school yearbook with pictures of my friends.

I also forgot my belt. During the bail hearing, I was escorted to the court in Belfast while handcuffed, walking with two escorting guards. They had to hold my trousers up on both sides, as they were too loose.

After a failed attempt at bail, I was transferred to Colnbrook detention centre near Heathrow. I felt hopeless, sort of numb. That's when I realised I was in the darkest place in my life, waiting to board a death flight with my fellow country women and men. I felt as if we were a herd of sheep, who had been selected and rounded up in a slaughterhouse, waiting day and night. The sheepdogs were the private contractors working for the Home Office, leading us into the darkness...

The whole place had the feel, appearance and smell of a jail. You share a bunk bed with a stranger who is as desperate as you are to figure out what's happening. The toilet in the room only had a curtain to separate it from the bunk bed – no privacy.

We all each got a plastic plate, small cereal bowl and plastic cutlery. You need to get used to the prison regime. Your doors open each morning for breakfast and you get locked up again after receiving food from the queue. The people who are serving and cooking food are also detainees – mostly long term, so you never want to displease them. You need to be friendly, otherwise you go without dinner. The environment is invested with powerplay and becomes very toxic. You share rooms with people who want to kill themselves.

You ask yourself: How much does Britain care about us?

I felt as if I had been thrown into a dark alleyway, where I couldn't do anything but wait.

That's when my friends across Northern Ireland rallied together to try and bring me back to Belfast. It was as if I was seeing the lights coming from the remaining cranes where the Titanic Ship had been built, and their reflection sparkled across the Giant's Causeway.

There was a united voice from both communities that had once been deeply divided. MPs from all the political parties, from Belfast South to East, from North to West. They all worked together and opened their hearts to help get me released from the horrors of detention. The feeling that there were people out their thinking about me during this period of limbo, is something that I can never explain. And nor will I ever forget it until my last breath.

My friends set up a campaign called 'Belfast needs Gee'. I'm still not sure why Belfast needed Gee. In fact, I left Belfast exactly a year after I received my Refugee Status to work for AVID*. One thing is for sure, I needed Belfast more than they needed me.

But I know that they didn't just do this for a random skinny guy with long hair and a funny name. They did this because they believed so deeply in humanitarian ideals – that home is not one place; home is where the heart is.

When I was released, it was a strange feeling going home, this time to Belfast. I felt that finally I belonged – somewhere safer and more inclusive.

I was transferred back to Larne, a rural part of Northern Ireland – the middle of nowhere. But when I walked out of the centre there, I felt that Northern Ireland was the most beautiful place on earth. I smelled the sweet scent of the air as I never had before.

I took the one hour journey back to Belfast. I was so tired, I kept falling asleep. I felt really dirty, like I needed to take a long hot shower. I arrived at the station and was hugged by three friends and four people who I had never met in my life.

In the following days, sometimes I would be out and I would hear my name from someone I didn't know and be greeted by them with lots of warm hugs. I felt like a rock star.

Detention reminded me that I am illegal because I am an immigrant. I grew up caught between the evils of racism, militarism, poverty and systematic oppression. But the people of Belfast came together and welcomed me as one of their own. I know there is often bad news coming out of Northern Ireland, but by doing a simple deed for me, a random stranger, they have shown that we are all equal. People can come together under a common purpose to address injustice.

I am still not sure if I agree with the sentence that charity begins at home. But I do feel that now I am home.

*AVID, the Association of Visitors to Immigration Detainees, was founded in 1994 in response to the increasing numbers of people being held in immigration detention, and the local community reaction to this. Find out more at: www.aviddetention.org.uk

Reibekuchen (Potato Cakes with Apple Compote)
Freddie – Germany

Ingredients

For the potato cakes:

2 onions, peeled

1 small bunch parsley

1kg firm potatoes

1tsp salt

A generous grind of black pepper

A pinch of ground nutmeg

2 medium free-range eggs, beaten.

200-300ml vegetable oil (such as sunflower or rapeseed oil)

For the apple compote:

800g Bramley cooking apples

3-4tbsp brown sugar

½tsp ground cinnamon

2-3tbsp sultanas (optional)

Serves 4

Method

Preheat the oven to 150°C/130°C Fan/Gas 2.

Finely dice the onions and wash and chop the parsley. Coarsely grate the potatoes into a colander over a bowl. Add a little salt and let them stand for 10-15 minutes, then squeeze out as much liquid as possible.

In the meantime, make the apple compote. Peel, core and dice the apples. Cook them on a medium-low heat with the sugar and a splash of water. Add the cinnamon and sultanas, if using, and simmer gently until apples have fallen apart, about 10-15 minutes. Add more sugar if necessary (Bramley apples can be very tart).

Tip the grated potatoes into a clean bowl and mix with the onions, parsley, salt, pepper, nutmeg and eggs.

Heat plenty of oil in a large frying pan over a medium heat. Place tablespoonfuls of the potato mix into the pan, pushing them down gently to flatten them. Fry in batches for about 6-8 minutes, gently turning over after 3-4 minutes once they are golden. Make sure they have enough space in the pan so that they cook properly.

Lift carefully out of pan with a spatula, placing on kitchen paper to soak up excess oil. Keep warm in the oven until all cakes are done.

Enjoy with some extra salt and pepper, if necessary, and lots of apple compote!

This is a variation of a very typical German dish, known as Reibekuchen or Kartoffelpuffer. It's a great dish for autumn or winter, and can be eaten cold. I remember eating heaps of them as a child, although then I was more keen on the sweet apple puree than the potato cakes. Now I like all of it!

Legend has it that when my dad was an undergraduate student in Cologne, this is one of the very few dishes he could cook. So he and his friends grated a lot of potatoes! You can replace some or all of the potatoes with other root vegetables like beetroot, parsnips or celariac. Instead of apple compote, you could serve them with smoked salmon and crème fraiche, or quark mixed with fresh herbs.

Why I volunteer

Freddie Seelig

I have always liked cooking, and it helps me to relax. Focussing on chopping that onion in front of me is my way of unwinding after a stressful day – call it culinary mindfulness! I also enjoy trying new dishes, and I have already tried several dishes at home that I came across through Stories & Supper.

Working with refugees and migrants forms a link to my own family's experience – my father and my grandparents had to flee their homes twice, and I can relate to the feeling of being separated from your hometown, your family and your friends (the German word 'Heimat' is very hard to translate). Cooking (and eating!) dishes from home helps us to keep a bond with our past and might ease any homesickness.

I am also a migrant, as I moved to the UK for work, but I could do so out of my own choice, and I realise I'm in a very privileged and fortunate position (despite the upheaval of Brexit). Volunteering with Stories & Supper helps to put things into perspective, as I learn about the dramatic and life-changing experiences of refugees. It has opened my eyes to the fact that their struggles are not over once they reach the UK, as they have to face the bureaucratic challenges of a hostile environment.

I can also connect with my local community of like-minded people and meet new friends. It allows me to give something back, and I feel privileged to participate in this project.

Shalinee Basak

I was attracted to volunteering with Stories & Supper because I feel very strongly about the negative immigration narrative in the public domain. My expectations have genuinely been exceeded throughout my volunteering experience with this group. I've had the privilege of hearing heart-rending stories from our refugee and asylum-seeker friends.

Getting to know each of them over the last year, as 'real' people with hopes, dreams and emotions has been extremely humbling. I've also come to appreciate the universality of human experience, most powerfully when we've bonded as a group over stories of different food from our respective homelands, sharing nostalgic experiences about smells, sights, sounds and tastes of food. That's what makes this book even more special in the way it brought our group together.

I truly believe Stories & Supper has begun to break stereotypes and challenge misleading labels about refugees and asylum seekers, by encouraging them to be vocal about their experiences. This has come to life in our supper clubs and other events where we've successfully reached people from various walks of life, to make these stories known.

As a volunteer, I continue to be amazed at the grit, resilience and determination of each person I've met. It inspires me to strive to challenge the status quo and get more and more of these voices heard every day.

Aswad Salad
Hawari – Sudan

HAWARI MADE THIS DELICIOUS AUBERGINE DIP FOR HIS SUPPER AT THE HORNBEAM CAFE IN WALTHAMSTOW

Ingredients

1kg aubergines
4tbsp of vegetable oil
3 cloves garlic, peeled
4tbsp lemon juice
1 green chilli
1tbsp mayonnaise (to taste)
2tbsp smooth peanut butter
170g plain yoghurt
1tsp ground black pepper
1tsp ground cumin

Serves 4 as a starter

Method

Peel the aubergines and cut into cubes. You can leave some of the skin on if you want more texture.

Heat the oil in a frying pan and fry the aubergine until it is cooked through and golden in places. You will need to do this in batches to avoid overcrowding the pan. Use more oil if necessary. Once fried, put the aubergines on kitchen paper to absorb the oil.

Place the fried aubergine in a bowl and mash with a fork. Grate the garlic and add to the bowl, along with the lemon juice. Mix.

Chop the chilli and add to the bowl with the mayonnaise, peanut butter, yogurt, pepper, cumin and oil. Mix well.

Taste and adjust the amount of lemon or salt as desired.

Serve with bread as part of a mezze.

Hawari was a head chef in Sudan and had two restaurants before he had to leave his country. He has cooked for two of our supper clubs, including making this delicious Aswad salad. Aswad means black in Arabic and refers to the colour of the aubergines.

Hawari finally got his Leave to Remain in late 2019 after waiting many years. He now hopes to open his own restaurant in London.

Workshop Dip
Olivia – UK

Ingredients

250g frozen broad beans
1tbsp of light tahini
A small handful of mint
Juice of half a lemon
A good pinch of salt
1 large clove of garlic, peeled
1tbsp of olive oil

Serves 4 as a side dish or starter

Method

First defrost the broad beans: Either leave them to defrost at room temperature, or soak in boiling water for five minutes then drain and leave to cool.

Place all the ingredients in a bowl and process with a stick blender, or place in a food processor. Blend until smooth.

Taste and adjust the amount of lemon, oil and salt, as you wish.

Serve with Turkish bread and a selection of mezze.

One of our Stories & Supper projects was called Global Story Cafés, *a collaboration with Queen Mary University in London. During the project we held storytelling and drama workshops every Saturday, always followed by eating a hearty lunch together. We would take turns to bring food each week, and one staple was green pea hummus, which we all loved. This is a broad bean version that has also become a firm favourite.*

Arepas
Laura – Venezuela

Ingredients

500ml cold water
1tsp corn oil
1tsp of salt
225g Harina PAN flour (or another brand of pre-cooked maize flour)

Makes about 8 depending on size

Method

Put the water, oil and salt in a medium bowl. Mix until the salt has dissolved. Slowly add the flour.

Mix with your hands, making circular movements and breaking any lumps that form with your fingers.

Let the dough rest for three minutes to thicken.

Preheat a non-stick 28cm square griddle pan over medium heat. If you don't have a griddle you can use a cast iron frying pan instead.

The dough should be firm enough to hold its shape without cracking when moulded. If it is too soft add a little more flour; if too dry add a little more water.

Form into balls and flatten them gently until they are patties about 1.25cm thick.

Place the arepas on the preheated griddle on a medium heat and cook for 5-7 minutes on each side or until lightly golden brown. Make sure they don't cook too quickly on the outside, as you want them to be properly cooked inside.

Split each arepa in half, spread butter inside and fill them with... whatever you like!

The arepa is one of our staple dishes in Venezuela. It is central to our culture and one of our higher culinary expressions. It is our daily bread. It brings families, friends and parties together. After I left my country my mum and my sister decided to save one day a week for eating arepas – they call it the Monday of the arepas.

Arepas are made with a white corn dough using maize flour. They can be fried, boiled or griddled in a flat, round cast iron pan we call a budare.

You can eat them any time – for breakfast, lunch or dinner. You can eat them hot or cold, fill them or use them like a bread roll or muffin. You can eat them with scrambled eggs, or cheese and ham. They go perfectly with chicken, beef, pork, tuna or beans. Some of my European friends even like them with chocolate or marmalade!

Laura – Venezuela

My name is Laura Isabel Martinez Da Silva. I'm from Venezuela and I've been living in London for two years. I studied Visual Media and I specialised in photography.

Venezuela is not a safe country, there is a lot of violence. I remember that when I lived there I couldn't take the camera out without someone reminding me that they were going to rob me, that I had to be careful. One day I decided to look for a photography Masters in Madrid and go to study. I applied and they selected me. They gave me a date and I started looking for a ticket to leave, always thinking that when I returned I could teach everything I had learned, share my passion and work in my area.

The day I said goodbye to my family, my parents, my friends and my boyfriend, my brothers, especially my twin sister, who I had never been away from before... that day, a part of me broke down and stayed in Venezuela, in my house. Yes, I left with the excitement of living a new adventure, meeting new people, studying, living alone... alone.

Once in Madrid, I began to enjoy everything that was unknown in my culture. This was another life. The Masters taught me so much about myself, that I realised how much I missed my family, my house, my sister. I remember one day, I came home from a class and did not stop crying. That day, the professor had asked me to show my latest project. I showed him a series of diptychs with photos of old spaces superimposed on new spaces, where only the emptiness lay and the people were no longer there. I know that when I said I had a twin, everyone was surprised. The professor told me that this was my project: how I managed to be away from someone I had been with for 28 years. That question left me speechless. I had not noticed until then how painful it was to think of that feeling of nostalgia, silence, loneliness and guilt. And I say guilt, because while my country was falling apart, I was enjoying, eating, being happy.

Calling my family became increasingly painful. Sad news was seen all the time on the news. People knew very little about what was happening in Venezuela, so they did not believe much of what I told them. Many people supported the politicians that destroyed my country. I simply kept silent and abandoned the conversations. It was very painful to know that I lived part of that and, as the situation got worse, my people were still there. I already knew that my trip would have no return.

One day my sister started sending me pictures of our house and how it looked now. I had the old photos of my earlier project and it occurred to me that we could do something together. She was there in the present and I was here in the past, alone and with memories. Little by little, we created a photo book, with a before and after, in the house where we grew up. And *Marta* was born.

Marta is the name of my house. It is of Hebrew origin and means lady. A home full of women where time has been responsible for demonstrating that everything is cyclical. Today we are, tomorrow, maybe not anymore. This was my final project in my Photography Masters. Some people learned about the situation of Venezuelans abroad. Others identified with the project because they, too, had had years without returning to their country, without being with their family, or even having them alive.

>

When I moved to London, I was struck again by the nostalgia of leaving another home behind, more so now that my sister had managed to move to Spain. We were together in Madrid for a few months, and then my plans to move to London with my partner began to happen.

Holding onto my little photo book of memories, *Marta*, I decided to apply for grants to give workshops about the family album. Photography is an interesting tool in the therapeutic process. It has helped me to move forward. Despite continually returning to the past, it helps you evaluate what you have and what is gone. To recognise that your home is you. The process of bringing back memories can be painful, but the result for me has been positive.

I have found that there's a lot of people that identify with me, with what I have been through and that I'm not alone. I didn't know what it felt like to be an immigrant, to have to abandon everything and start from scratch somewhere else, with no one. Everyone who is in Stories & Supper in some way or another has lost something. I could identify with them, I could value my situation more, I could be thankful for where I am today.

We are all immigrants. We all have a story to tell. The important thing is that we recognise in our own history that we were brave and strong to get where we are today.

Yaprak Sarması (Meat-Stuffed Vine Leaves)
Filiz – Turkey

Ingredients

300g fresh vine leaves (or one jar of preserved leaves)

2 medium onions, peeled

1 small bunch of parsley

2 medium tomatoes

100g rice

400g beef or lamb mince

1tbsp tomato paste

50ml water

Salt

Black pepper

Chilli/red pepper flakes, to taste

3tbsp oil or butter, or a mix of both

Plain yoghurt, to serve

Method

If using fresh leaves, blanch in boiling water for five minutes, depending on the tenderness of the leaves. Refresh in cold water. Gently squeeze the water out of the leaves and separate, taking care not to damage or tear them. If using preserved leaves, soak and wash them, changing the water a few times. Depending on the brand, you may need to blanch them for a minute if they seem tough. Cut the stems off the leaves.

Chop the onions and parsley very finely. Grate or blend the tomatoes. Wash the rice. Place the onions, parsley, tomatoes and rice in a large bowl with the mince, half of the tomato paste and the water. Season with salt, pepper and chilli/pepper flakes, to taste. Mix well.

Add the oil or butter and the remaining tomato paste to a pan or pot with a lid and gently fry the tomato paste until it is bright red and shiny.

Place the leaves on a flat surface. Cut any leaf that is too large into two. Take a teaspoon or two of the meat and rice mixture depending on the size of the leaf and place on the widest part of the leaf, leaving a thin strip empty at the bottom. Fold the bottom of the leaf over the meat, and carry on rolling, tucking in the sides as you go. Repeat with the remaining leaves.

Place the stuffed leaves snugly in the pan with the tomato paste. When the bottom of the pan is covered, carry on with a second layer. Add just enough water to cover the leaves. Ideally, cover with a heavy, heatproof plate to stop them from moving around as they cook, then cover with the lid. Bring to the boil, reduce heat to low and cook for about 40 minutes.

Carefully remove the lid and the plate and check to make sure the leaves are soft and the rice and meat are cooked. Serve with yoghurt.

Stuffed vegetables are a favourite for us in Turkey. Peppers, aubergines, courgettes or cabbage leaves can all be stuffed with a meat filling to be eaten hot, or a rice and olive oil filling to be eaten cold. But the greatest is always the stuffed vine leaves. It works better with fattier mince and you can use beef or lamb, or a mixture. The vine leaves can be substituted with chard or collard greens as well. It is fiddly but well worth the effort, and is one of the dishes I miss most from home.

Yalıncı Dolma (Vegetarian Stuffed Vine Leaves)
Helen & Nesrin – Cyprus

Ingredients

30 to 40 fresh vine leaves (or one jar of preserved leaves)

250g basmati or long-grain rice

1 large onion, peeled

2 large vine tomatoes

250g hellim/halloumi cheese

2tbsp dried mint

freshly ground pepper

150ml olive oil

2 lemons

Method

If using fresh vine leaves, wash them, remove the stalks and blanch in batches in boiling water for a minute or so. They will turn from bright green to a dull olive colour. Lift out carefully with a slotted spoon and leave in a colander to drain. If using preserved leaves, soak and wash them, changing the water a few times. If they seem tough, blanch them for a minute as above.

Soak the rice in hot water for 15 minutes. Rinse with cold water and drain thoroughly. Peel and finely chop the onion. Grate the cheese. Cut each tomato in half and coarsely grate. Put the rice, onion, tomato, cheese and mint in a large bowl. Season with pepper. The cheese should provide enough salt.

Line a large pan with any broken vine leaves to prevent the dolmas from sticking. Lay your first vine leaf on the work surface, vein side up with the stalk end pointing towards you. Place a heaped teaspoon of filling in a sausage shape across the bottom end of the leaf, leaving a gap at either side. Roll up the bottom of the leaf then fold in both sides to cover the filling. Continue rolling until you have a neat parcel.

Roll all the vine leaves in the same way. Place each one into the pan, packing them tightly as you go. When you have used all the filling and leaves, make sure the pan is packed tightly and cover the top with a few more broken vine leaves and one lemon, sliced.

Combine the olive oil with an equal amount of hot water and the juice of the other lemon and pour over the vine leaves. Place an old heavy plate on top of the vine leaves to weigh them down and cover with a lid.

Cook on a low heat for about one hour, or until the rice is cooked. You may need to top up the water during cooking.

Serve at room temperature with yoghurt.

Helen

This is another Turkish Cypriot recipe inherited from my mother-in-law Nesrin. They are called Yalıncı Dolma, which translates as liar dolma, as they don't contain meat – but you wouldn't know it to look at them. The addition of the Cypriot hellim/halloumi cheese adds extra flavour and carnivores have been known to admit that they prefer them to the meat version.

These are best made with fresh vine leaves, if you have any Cypriot neighbours who will share some from their garden. Pick young medium-sized vine leaves – if they are too big or too old they will be tough, if they are too small you won't be able to put enough filling in them. To make these vegan, you can leave out the cheese and increase the amount of rice.

Dolma with Lamb and Potatoes
Abdullah – Kurdistan

Ingredients

20 fresh vine leaves (or taken from a jar of preserved leaves)

2 aubergines

2 courgettes

2 large onions, peeled

2tsp vegetable oil

12 lamb ribs (or a rack of lamb cut into invidual pieces)

Salt and black pepper

¼tsp garlic powder

¼tsp ground ginger

4 large tomatoes

250g long-grain rice

1 large potato, peeled

A handful of broad beans

2 lemons

Serves 6 to 8

Method

Prepare the vine leaves by blanching or washing them, as you would for Yalıncı Dolma (page 51). Top and tail and hollow out the aubergines and courgettes, then cut them in half so you have short cylinders. Make a hole in one of the onions, by removing its centre.

Chop the second onion, then fry gently in the oil. Add the ribs and brown for a minute or so. Add a pinch of salt, some black pepper, the garlic powder and ginger. Add water to just cover the meat, place a lid on the pan and cook on a low heat for 25 minutes.

Meanwhile, make the dolma: Wash the rice and drain. Chop the tomato very finely and add to the rice. Season well with salt and pepper.

Take a vine leaf and place it vein side up, wide end towards you. Place a spoonful of rice mix at the bottom end and roll up into a cigar shape, tucking in the sides as you go. Repeat with all the vine leaves. Then use the remaining rice to losely stuff the vegetables.

Cut the potato into thick slices and lay on the bottom of a large pot. Stand the stuffed vegetables upright in the pot, then fit the lamb and onions in around the vegetables. Scatter over the the broad beans and place the stuffed vine leaves on top. Pack tightly. Add the liquid used to cook the lamb, then top up with enough water to just cover everything.

Put a lid on the pot and cook on a very low heat for about 40 to 50 minutes, checking to see if the rice is done. Add more water during cooking if needed. Serve with a squeeze of lemon and flat bread.

This is my mum's recipe – she would cook it twice a week, especially on Fridays. For some reason my brothers didn't like it, but I always loved it. You have to prepare the pot carefully, so that everything is fitted in properly together and it all looks nice.

Abdullah – Kurdistan

I was born in Kurdistan in 1988. I lived in a city in a big house with three floors. I lived with my parents and my two older sisters and three older brothers. I am the youngest – the baby of the family!

My family are very religious, strict Muslim. I was as well when I lived there, but after I left, I changed my mind. I believe in God, but I don't believe in religion. I'm not against my religion, but I don't want to follow something which doesn't make sense to me. But this was a problem for my family.

When I was a child, I used to play marbles – I loved it so much. It was like my god, my other family! I was so addicted. I would play with my friends in the neighbourhood. When I got older, I used to play snooker with my friends. I still like to play snooker here. I like football too, not watching it but playing it when I can.

I miss the food from home so much. My mum used to do the cooking. She had so much experience. Sometimes I try to cook things that she used to make - like dolma - but it never tastes as good. I can cook, but not like my mum. She took a lot of time over it. She mixed rice with many things. Onion, garlic, different herbs and flavours, like saffron. Saffron's not expensive in my country. Here I don't have time to cook. And I don't like to take a lot of time when I cook for myself.

Back home we have two Eids. For Eid al-Ahda, there is a tradition called Qurban, where we cut the head off the animal and you give to poor people. And in Ramadam, you fast for 30 days and then celebrate. It's really fun. We visit people, our relatives, everyone does. In the mornings, you eat. Not a light meal, a heavy meal – at 5am! And then at dusk you eat again. You don't eat anything all day. You don't drink either. And you can't do anything bad, so you shouldn't lie or anything like that. That's a good thing about our religion. Every religion has good and bad. The final meal for Eid is everything. It's very special. In preparation, my mum wouldn't sleep all night. She cooked soups, beans, okra, many things.

I lived in Kurdistan for 25 years, and then I left. I arrived in the UK in 2015. The reason I left is complicated. It's a long story. I had a relationship that was not accepted in my country. I was not allowed to marry the girl that I loved.

My journey here was long. First, I went to Italy, then to France, then Belgium and then I came here. From Turkey to Italy it took almost six days in a ship. For three days we didn't have enough food because we were 75 people in one small room. You couldn't even sit down, you had to stand sideways. If you put your feet out, they would be on someone else. One night I fainted and when I woke up, there were five people on top of me. I almost died. And it was so dirty, we didn't have food or water. We drank the water from the ocean. It was so bad for our stomachs, but we had no choice for five and a half days, almost six days!

And when we arrived in Italy it was so good because we could all lie down on the beach. And people brought food for us. But then the police came and took our fingerprints, which

>

was a problem for me when I arrived in the UK. They said I needed to go back to Italy because I had given my fingerprints there. But they didn't send me back. I was so lucky that they accepted my story and let me stay.

Travelling through France and Italy was a bit easier. I travelled by train, but without a passport. I bought the ticket but they refused me. They said "where is your passport?" Many times I tried, but I didn't give up. You can find a time in the early morning, or at night - just a short time. From France, I came by lorry. We were four people. One of them opened the door to the lorry and we all got in. It was hard but I was determined to arrive in the UK, because I knew I would have a better life here.

But here in the UK it has been really hard. I've had bad experiences. Very bad. One of my brothers had been living over here, in Warwickshire. When I first arrived and was taken to a detention centre, they said to me, "We should take you back to Italy because that's where you gave your fingerprints, but if you give us his address we might release you." My brother didn't want to give his address. He had made some bad friends in the past. He doesn't feel for his family.

I didn't want to go back to Italy because they don't support you, or give you food or accommodation. When they released me I was so happy. I could open a new page, make a new life. But when I arrived at my brother's house, which belonged to his girlfriend, he kicked me out after one week. After one week. I didn't speak English and I didn't have anything. No money, no accommodation, no friends. It was so hard. I went to the Home Office and I asked for accommodation. They said, "no, you have an address".

This lasted for three years, it was so hard. Some nights I stayed on the street. And when I found jobs, people would pay me less than a car wash or a take away because I was not allowed to work. But what could I do? I couldn't survive myself – I had no choice. But I made some friends, they helped me and I didn't give up. I believed in myself. And I was always chasing my case. I went to lots of different charities, I really appreciated them for many things. After three years, the Home Office let me register as an asylum seeker and gave me accommodation. But I still wasn't allowed to work or study. You are not allowed to study if you're an asylum seeker. You feel like giving up.

Then, finally the court accepted me as a refugee, in the summer of 2019. And now my life is completely different. Now I have my refugee status I can do many things, like driving lessons. I'm doing the theory now. I could make a lot of money with driving. And I'm planning to get a lorry. I used to drive for five years in my country. I'm a good driver. And I could drive a lorry here as well. It could change my life.

"After three years, the Home Office let me register as an asylum seeker. But I still wasn't allowed to work or study. You feel like giving up."

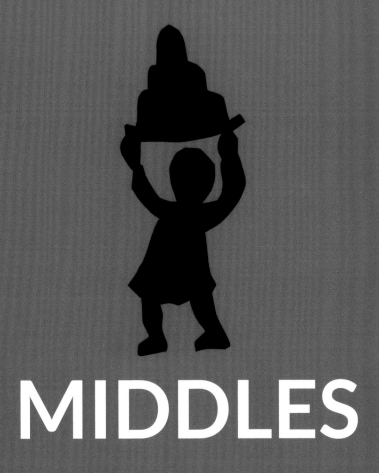

MIDDLES

Paneer Curry
Shahnaz – India

WE SERVED THIS AT OUR STREET FOOD & STORIES POP-UP AT THE WALTHAMSTOW GARDEN PARTY – AND SOLD OUT!

Ingredients

300g paneer	¼tsp ground turmeric
250g fresh tomatoes	1tsp chilli powder, depending on taste
1 large onion, peeled	1tbsp ground coriander
5 cloves garlic, peeled	2 whole green chillies
A thumb-sized piece of ginger, peeled	4tbsp natural yoghurt
4tbsp sunflower oil	1tbsp dry fenugreek leaves
50g cashew nuts	1tbsp butter or ghee
3 cardamom pods	Salt, to taste
6 cloves	3tbsp single cream (optional)
2 bay leaves	Small handful fresh coriander
1 small cinnamon stick	

Serves 4 to 6

Method

Cut the paneer into 2cm cubes. Finely chop the tomatoes and onion. Crush the garlic and grate the ginger.

In a small frying pan, heat 1tbsp of the oil, then add the onions, cashews, garlic, ginger, cardamom, cloves, bay leaves and cinnamon. Cook for 5 minutes, then add the tomatoes, turmeric, chilli powder and ground coriander. Remove the cinnamon and blend the onions, tomatoes and spices to a paste with a stick blender.

In a large pan, heat the remaining 3tbsp of oil. Add the tomato and onion puree and cook for 5 to 10 minutes. Add about 250ml water and the green chillies and cook for a further 5 minutes. Lower the heat. Add the yoghurt, mixing it in slowly so that it doesn't curdle.

This recipe belongs to North India – people in Delhi and Bombay love paneer. They will eat paneer with everything – peas, spinach, there is even a dish called butter paneer.

Grind the dry fenugreek leaves into a powder in a pestle and mortar and add to the pot. Add salt, to taste. Cook for a further 3 to 5 minutes.

In a separate pan, fry the paneer in butter or ghee until golden. Add the paneer to the sauce and cook on a low heat for 5 mins until it bubbles.

Lower the heat and cover the pan, cooking until the oil rises to the top, or for about 10 minutes. Add the cream, if using, and stir.

Pick and wash a handful of coriander leaves and scatter on the top of the curry. Serve with plain basmati rice.

Bagara Baingan (Aubergine Curry)
Shahnaz – India

Ingredients

50g tamarind block

15 cashew nuts

50g peanuts

2tbsp tahini

2 onions, peeled

5tbsp sunflower oil

1 bulb of garlic

4cm piece of ginger, peeled

½tsp turmeric

2tsp ground cumin

2tsp ground coriander

1tsp ground fenugreek

A handful of fresh curry leaves

1tsp chilli powder, or to taste

1kg small aubergines (or
regular aubergines)

Salt to taste

Fresh coriander leaves

Serves 4 to 6

Method

Soak the tamarind in 150ml of boiling water for 10 minutes, or until the water is cool enough to handle.

Meanwhile, dry fry the cashews and peanuts in a hot pan without oil and remove from the pan. Cube the onions. Add 2tbsp of oil to the pan and fry the onions for a few minutes until they are half cooked. Remove.

Separate the garlic cloves and peel. Roughly chop the ginger. Blend the garlic and ginger with a little water until it forms a paste.

Add the remaining oil to the pan, followed by the turmeric, cumin, ground coriander, fenugreek, curry leaves, chilli powder, and the ginger and garlic paste. Fry for a few minutes.

Make deep slits into the side of each small aubergine along its length, but don't cut through. If you are using regular aubergines, cut them in half widthways and then cut each half into four wedges. Add the aubergines to the spices and fry for 10 minutes, or until they start to soften.

Blend the nuts, tahini and onions together with a stick blender, with 250ml of water. Add to the pan and cook for 10-15 minutes over a medium heat. Add a good pinch of salt, to taste.

Squeeze the tamarind, discarding the pulp and seeds, until you have about 125ml of tamarind water. Add to the pan. Add a bit more water if needed. Cook for a further 10 to 15 minutes, until the oil rises.

Scatter with fresh coriander leaves and serve with basmati rice.

This recipe comes from Hyderabad, South India – it is a royal curry. My mum's aubergine curry was very tasty, so this recipe reminds me of back home.

Shahnaz made this curry for our supper in Ledbury, Herefordshire in 2018. It has since become a favourite with the team and has a wonderful depth of flavour. It uses the small thin aubergines (about 10cm long) you can find in Asian or African shops, rather than the larger regular aubergines you find in the supermarket. If you use regular aubergines you can cut them into large wedges.

Sambar
Shahnaz – India

Ingredients

100g toor dal
50g block tamarind (with seeds)
1 carrot
1 onion, peeled
2 small or 1 regular aubergine
5-6 large okra
½ kaddu (bottle gourd)
1 small bunch of coriander
5 cloves of garlic, peeled
2 large tomatoes

1tbsp cumin seeds
½tsp ground turmeric
Salt, to taste
5-6 curry leaves
1tsp fenugreek seeds
1tsp mustard seeds
1tsp ground coriander
5-6 green chillies
3 tbsp vegetable oil

Method

Soak the toor dal for one hour before you start.

Cover the tamarind with boiling water and leave to soak.

Meanwhile, cut the carrot, onion, aubergines, okra and kaddu into large pieces. Wash and chop the coriander. Slice two of the cloves of garlic. Roughly chop the tomatoes.

Drain and rinse the toor dal. Boil in 300ml water with half a teaspoon of cumin seeds, the unsliced garlic, the turmeric and salt to taste, over a medium heat. Boil until the dal is soft, for about one hour (or cook in a pressure cooker for 10 minutes). Blend with a stick blender.

Squeeze the juice out the tamarind and discard the pulp and seeds. Add the tamarind liquid to the dal.

Heat the oil in a large pan and fry the carrot, onion, aubergine and kaddu with the sliced garlic, curry leaves, fenugreek seeds, mustard seeds, ground coriander, green chillies and the rest of the cumin seeds over a medium heat, for about 10 minutes. Add the chopped tomatoes and fry for another couple of minutes.

Add the dal to the vegetables and stir. Cook for a further 15-20 minutes, until the oil rises to the surface.

Scatter over the coriander leaves and serve.

This is a South Indian dish, which is usually eaten for breakfast. It's very healthy and full of vitamins. We serve it with Idli (savoury rice cakes) and Upma (a semolina porridge).

Suleiman – Sudan

In Sudan I lived in a village. It was not very big. All the buildings were made of wood and near the village there was a big river. We drank water from the river. You had to keep it for a few days at home until it settled and became clean.

We grew tomatoes and a lot of vegetables. In summer there were mangoes, guava and lemon. The mangoes and guavas smelled sweet. You could grow a lot of fruit there. Autumn is the rainy season and we grew many things. Meat was our favourite food, with aseeda. We also ate bamya (okra) with kisra, a type of pancake.

We knew everyone in the neighbourhood. Our culture was the same. Uncles, granduncles, everyone was like family. In the evening, there would be a lot of people in the neighbourhood, all talking in the road. Your neighbours with their two children, three children, all telling stories and laughing. When you had to go to your land, you would tell everyone in the village and people would come and help you. When you needed anything, people would come and help you. You wouldn't do it alone.

I left my village in 2003. The Janjaweed came to attack the village and killed a lot of people. They attacked everything in the village. Everyone had to move to a nearby town. I spent 12 years in that town. I started a business where people could come and charge their phones and pay me for it. But then people from the Government started saying that I supported the opposition. They beat me and put me in prison for a day.

Our Chief came and spoke to us. He said the Government were accusing the Masalit tribe of supporting the opposition. We had to stay within a certain area and go to sign in every week. They would question me to see if I had any information about the opposition. Then they said they would kill me. I told my uncle. He told me I had to go and he helped me to leave Sudan.

I left Sudan on 27th July 2015. I had no documents. I got to Libya on 10th September.

I spent four months in a Libyan prison. In Libya they arrest you and put you in prison and you have to pay to get out. They let you go, but then arrest you again. After prison I spent five months working in Libya. Libya is very dangerous. When you go outside, shopping or anything, it's very dangerous. Sometimes they take everything – your money, your clothes, your phone. They are killing Black people.

Libyans will take you across the sea if you give them money. I worked for five months to earn enough. A Sudanese man had given me the money to get out of prison. So first I paid him back and then I paid about £800 to go in a boat. It was a dinghy. There were about 100 of us. Was I scared? What can you do? When we were in the middle of the sea, a European organisation with a big ship took us all on board for two days and we disembarked in Italy.

I spent seven days in Italy. A lot of people were living in a park. There was no food and no drink. Some people brought us sandwiches. It was the season for rain. From Italy I went to   >

France. I just took the train. When the inspector came, I hid in the toilet. I came to France on the 20th June 2016 and made it to Calais. I stayed in the Jungle.

In Calais the traffic was very busy. One night when all the lorries stopped in the road, I climbed in one. It was 2am. You don't know where the lorries are going. It could be Belgium or anywhere. I was alone in the lorry. It went on a train and in the morning I found myself in the UK. It was the 2nd August. The lorry parked inside a big compound and the people working there saw me and called the police.

The police came and put me in handcuffs and took me to a police station. I spent 24 hours at the police station. They interviewed me and then took me to a hostel. I was there for seven days. After that, I was moved to Liverpool for one month. Then they moved me to Ilford and from Ilford to Dagenham, where I lived in a house with four other people while I waited to get my papers.

In my first interview I was questioned about my illegal entry to the UK. I was very tired, very confused. I didn't understand what was being said. Although the interpreter spoke Arabic it was not my dialect. I must have given many answers that were not correct because I didn't understand what they were asking. This caused me many problems.

In 2017 my case came before the court. Again, I was asked many complicated questions that I didn't understand. When I replied, they said I was lying because what I was saying was different from my first interview. I was confused. I had difficulties again with the interpreter they gave me. I did not understand much of what they were asking. My application was turned down.

I appealed and I finally got Leave to Remain in November 2018. Now I go to college to improve my English and I am looking for a job. I don't mind what work I do.

In Sudan it was very dangerous. In Libya it was very dangerous. But here people are very friendly. When you go to an organisation they help you. Nobody is shouting at you in the road. You have freedom here. Nobody is saying: "You're Black, you're African." Nobody is saying this. In England it is safe. In other countries the people and the government are not good for refugees. I feel very safe in the UK.

Kho-Suey
Mariam Siddiqui – Burma

MARIAM COOKED A VEGAN VERSION OF KHO-SUEY FOR ONE OF OUR SUPPER CLUBS, USING SEITAN INSTEAD OF CHICKEN.
TO MAKE THIS RECIPE VEGAN REPLACE THE CHICKEN WITH SEITAN AND LEAVE OUT THE EGGS.

This dish is a favourite amongst the Burmese and Muslim Indian Burmese community. It is usually made with chicken and there are many possible variations, depending on individual and family taste. This version of the recipe is my mother's and when I was a child it was always associated with the family eating together and telling stories. We always made extra to be shared amongst my extended family.

I'm pleased to share this much-loved recipe which has been passed down through three generations. It's like sharing a bit of our history and the journey of our family with others to enjoy.

Kho-Suey is traditionally served with the large bowl of curry in the middle of the tray, surrounded by its accompaniments. The idea is that each person takes as much as they like into their own bowl, adding extras according to their taste.

Ingredients
Tomato Chicken Curry
1 medium onion, peeled
3-4 garlic cloves, peeled
3cm piece of fresh ginger, peeled
1 fresh lemongrass stalk
3-4 kaffir lime leaves
400g tin tomatoes (or 5-6 medium tomatoes)
2-4tbsp vegetable oil
1tsp chilli powder
½tsp ground turmeric
1kg boneless chicken
Salt to taste

Coconut soup
1 small onion, peeled
3-4 spring onions
1-2 green chillies (optional)
2tbsp chickpea flour
250g tin coconut milk
250ml water
4-6 whole peppercorns
Salt to taste

Accompaniments
500g spaghetti
1 onion, peeled
3 garlic cloves, peeled
3tbsp sunflower oil
2 samosa or filo sheets
2 free-range eggs
1 bunch coriander
1 lemon

Serves five

Method
Tomato Chicken Curry
Add the onion, garlic, ginger, lemongrass, lime leaves and tomatoes to the bowl of a food processor and blend to a puree (making sure the lemongrass is properly blended).

Add the oil to a saucepan, then the puree and cook on a medium heat for 5 minutes.

Add the dry spices and leave to simmer on a medium heat, until the oil rises.

Cut the chicken into cubes, add to the curry and cook with the lid on for 30 minutes on a low heat, adding a bit of water if necessary. Once cooked, set aside to cool.

Coconut Soup
Chop the onions, the spring onions and the chillies if using.

In a medium pan, dry roast the chickpea flour until golden and transfer to a bowl. Gradually whisk in the coconut milk and water (as if making a batter).

Pour the soup into the pan and then add both onions, the chillies and pepper. Bring to the boil, then reduce the heat to a simmer, adding more water if necessary. Cook for 15 minutes.

Accompaniments

Boil the spaghetti according to packet instructions, drain and set aside.

Slice the garlic and onion. Fry both separately in the oil until golden and crispy. Drain on kitchen paper.

Fry the samosa pastry sheets until crunchy, then transfer to kitchen paper.

Boil the eggs for 10 minutes, run under cold water to cool. Then peel and slice.

Finely chop the coriander and cut the lemon into eight wedges.

Transfer accompaniments to small bowls to serve.

Cook-Up Rice
Winnie – Guyana

Ingredients

200g dried black-eyed beans (or a 400g tin)	2-4 whole wiri wiri (Guyana) peppers, or other hot chillies such as scotch bonnet
10 chicken wings	1tbsp vegetable oil
Sea salt, to taste	500g brown basmati rice
Freshly ground black pepper	400g tin coconut milk
1 onion, peeled	1 bay leaf
3-4 garlic cloves, peeled	2 chicken stock cubes
1 small bunch dried thyme sprigs	

Serves 6 to 8

Method

Soak the beans in cold water overnight, if using dried beans.

Cut the chicken wings in half, rub with salt and pepper and leave for an hour. Finely chop the onion and garlic. Rub the sprigs of dried thyme to remove the leaves and discard the stems. For more heat, chop the chillies.

If using dried beans, place in a medium saucepan, cover with water and boil on a high heat for 10 minutes. Then reduce the heat and cook for another 20 minutes until almost cooked. Drain.

In a large saucepan, heat the oil. Then fry the chicken gently until it is brown. Add the onions, garlic and thyme and fry for a couple of minutes.

Add the rice, coconut milk, chilli peppers, bay leaf, stock cubes, about 500ml of boiling water and the cooked beans to the pan with the chicken. Bring to the boil, then lower the heat and simmer.

Cover the pot with a lid and leave to cook for 35 to 40 minutes, until all the water has evaporated and the rice and chicken are cooked, adding more water if necessary during cooking.

Variations

To make with fish instead of chicken: Make rice as above, leaving out the chicken. Season the fish, then fry until cooked and serve on the rice.

For a vegetarian option: Make the rice as above, leaving out the chicken and replacing the chicken stock cube with vegetable bouillon powder. Peel and slice 3 yellow plantain, fry in vegetable oil and serve on the rice.

This is a Guyanese recipe where everything is cooked in one pot. My grandma Philomena Shako used to cook it every Saturday. It was a different dish each day: Cook-Up Rice on Saturday, soup on Sunday. She always used to say, "waste not, want not".

My grandma was the head of the family. All her children moved to the city, so her grandchildren went to live with her. We lived in the countryside with chickens and donkeys, the whole village was our playground.

I always wanted to eat with my grandma. I wanted to sit on her lap so she would feed me. I would turn away and say, 'I won't eat it', so that my grandma would feed me. My grandpa would always be given the biggest portion, the finest cuts of meat, because he was out working.

This dish reminds me of my grandma, it's real comfort food.

Chicken Biryani
Shahnaz – India

HYDERABAD IS FAMOUS FOR THIS DISH, WHICH IS SERVED AT WEDDINGS. THERE IS A SAYING – 'WITHOUT BIRYANI, THERE IS NO PARTY'

Ingredients

For the marinade:

2 lemons

2 thumb-sized pieces of ginger, peeled

7-8 cloves of garlic, peeled

2-3 green chillies, or to taste

3 cloves

1tbsp dry fenugreek leaves

½ large bunch mint leaves

½ large bunch coriander leaves

250g yoghurt

1tbsp ground coriander

1-2 large cinnamon sticks

3 cardamom pods

2 bay leaves

1tbsp chilli powder

¼tsp ground nutmeg

½tsp black cumin

1 large onion, peeled

125ml vegetable oil or ghee

500g boneless chicken thighs

For the rice:

500g basmati rice

2 cloves

2 cardamom pods

½tsp black cumin

2tsp salt, or to taste

1-2tbsp vegetable oil

1-2tbsp ghee (optional)

Serves 6

Method

First prepare the marinade: Juice the lemons.

Blend the ginger, garlic and green chillies into a paste using a stick blender, adding a splash of water if necessary.

Grind the cloves and fenugreek leaves in a pestle and mortar.

Wash and chop most of the mint and coriander leaves, leaving a small handful of each for the rice.

Mix all of the above ingredients with the yogurt, ground coriander, cinnamon sticks, cardamom pods, bay leaves, chilli powder, ground nutmeg and black cumin.

Finely chop the onion and fry in the oil or ghee for about 15 minutes or until starting to brown. Then add the onion with the oil or ghee to the marinade.

Cut the chicken into large cubes and add to the marinade and leave for 1 hour.

Meanwhile, prepare the rice: Wash the rice in three or four changes of water. Cover with boiling water and leave to soak for 30 minutes.

Bring 1 litre of water to the boil in a pan and add the cloves, cardamom pods, black cumin, the reserved coriander and mint leaves, the salt and oil. Drain the rice and add it to the pan.

Boil the rice for exactly 6 minutes. Drain.

Transfer the chicken and its marinade to the bottom of a large, deep pot. Cover with the drained rice. Place the pot over a high heat. If you want more flavour, add 1-2tbsp ghee.

Cover the pot really well, no steam should be able to escape. If necessary, cover the pan with foil before putting on the lid. Sealing the pan is traditionally done with pastry (made from atta flour, cumin, ginger, garlic and baking soda), which can also be eaten.

Cook on a high heat for 10 minutes, then turn the heat to low. After a few more minutes, check if the rice is done by putting a metal knife into the middle of the pan. If there is still water in the pan, cook for a few more minutes until the rice is ready.

At the end of the cooking time, stir to mix the chicken and the rice. Serve with raita.

Nokaw (Lamb and Chickpea Soup)
Abdullah – Kurdistan

Ingredients

125g dried chickpeas

1 onion, peeled

3 garlic cloves, peeled

50g kidney fat (or 3tbsp vegetable oil)

500g lamb (ribs, shank or chops)

½tsp chilli powder

½tsp ground turmeric

Salt, to taste

2 dried limes

Serves 4

Method

Soak the chickpeas in plenty of water overnight. Rinse in clean water. Drain.

Chop the onion and garlic finely.

Put an empty pressure cooker on the heat for 2 minutes. Add the kidney fat and wait until it melts before adding the lamb, or add the oil and heat. Fry the meat until brown. Add the onion and garlic and cook until lightly browned.

Carefully add 1 litre hot water, the chickpeas, chilli, turmeric and salt. Make several small holes in each of the dried limes and add to the pan.

Place the pressure cooker lid on securely, increase the pressure over a high heat and then turn the heat to low and cook for 40 minutes. Gradually reduce the pressure before opening.

To cook without a pressure cooker, bring the soup to a boil, without adding the chickpeas. Then simmer in a covered pan on a low heat for about 2 hours 30 minutes. While the lamb is cooking, boil the chickpeas on a high heat for 10 minutes, then add to the soup for the last 45 minutes of its cooking time.

Serve with soft bread rolls.

This is a very famous Kurdish recipe, but everyone makes a different version. My mum would make this once a week back home. When I moved here, I called her on the phone and she taught me how to make it. Ribs are the best thing to cook with chickpeas – they make the dish more delicious.

When I cooked Nokaw for the first time I didn't know how long to cook it for and when I opened the pan it was completely dry. I put more water in, but it had lost the taste. And sometimes I forget to soak the chickpeas the night before so I can't make it.

I make it for myself every two weeks now. It's so delicious. When I invite friends over they always ask me to cook it for them.

Bengali Aloo Posto
(Potato in Poppy Seed Paste)
Shalinee – India

Ingredients

3-4tbsp white poppy seeds (posto or
khus-khus)
4 medium potatoes, peeled
2 green chillies
1tbsp mustard oil
1½tbsp nigella seeds (kalonji or kala jeera)
Salt to taste
A pinch of sugar
1tsp butter or ghee (clarified butter)

Method

Soak the poppy seeds in a cup of warm water for about an hour. Drain and grind the seeds to a smooth paste in a pestle and mortar or in a blender. Add a tablespoon or more of water while grinding if paste gets too thick.

Cut the potatoes into small cubes. Slice the green chilies, discarding the seeds if you don't want it to be too spicy.

Heat the mustard oil in a pan and add the nigella seeds once the oil is hot.

Fry for a few minutes and then add the sliced green chillies stirring as they start to sputter.

Now add the cut potatoes and cook on a medium heat until the potatoes brown, stirring often. Add the salt and a small pinch of sugar.

Add the poppy seed paste at this point, making sure to cover all the potatoes evenly. Cook for a few minutes before adding 250ml of water.

Simmer and keep covered for 10-12 minutes until the potatoes are cooked through. The mixture should be thick and the poppy seeds paste should be sticking to the potato pieces.

Add the butter or ghee and allow to melt while leaving on low heat.

Aloo Posto is best served with very hot plain white rice.

The opium poppy, from which posto – khus khus or poppy seeds – are derived, was originally cultivated during the Mughal rule in India. When India was colonised, the British soon discovered a huge market for illegal opium in China after the Battle of Plassey in 1757, when they set up base in Bengal.

Posto soon entered every Bengali home, starting in eastern Bengal (now Bangladesh) from where my grandparents fled during the Partition of India in 1947, as they migrated to West Bengal in India.

It was a staple during hot summers at lunchtime when I was growing up. My grandmother cooked it with potatoes, yams or colocassia, also with vegetables such as okra, gourds or aubergines.

We Bengalis are known for our afternoon siesta, so I have fond memories of eating aloo posto with hot rice and napping afterwards. My grandmother joked that these long naps had nothing to do with the poppy seeds' narcotic properties!

If you can't get white poppy seeds, you can use black ones.

Mary – Ghana

I was born in Accra, Ghana, in 1961. I lived with my mum and dad, three sisters and two brothers.

The weather is very nice there. It's hot. You can enjoy it, you can sleep out. When it rained, people would bathe in the rain. I loved it. Here we don't see people enjoying the rain. They are going somewhere and if it's raining, they just run to get out of it. In Africa, because there is so much sun, when it's raining, we love it. We just stand there, bathing in the rain. It makes me so happy. And the little ones also come and bathe in the rain.

In Accra, the weather is hot, but the living is hard. If you don't have a good job, it is not easy for you to enjoy the life there. So many things have happened there. Sometimes people hear about other places and say, "Oh what a nice country!" But inside, there are things going on.

When you're with your family, it is a very happy time, a sacred time. When you don't have your family, it is very hard. Family is the most important thing. They are with you so that you can make a life together.

My parents tried their best to support us, to help. But sometimes things were hard, especially for the women. My mother had to bring up five children. My father was a shoemaker and my mother used to sell yams in the market. She did it to support our family. When there were leftovers, she brought them home and cooked them for us. So I really enjoyed eating yam.

When my mother cooked, we helped her and then we would eat together. We didn't divide the food, we would eat together from one bowl. If it is in separate bowls you think, "Oh I won't get enough!" But if you eat together, then everybody will feel fuller.

If there wasn't enough money to buy chairs, you would put mats on the floor and then all sit together and fold your legs. And we would just start eating slowly, using our hands.

One funny thing is that if there is meat, the mother cuts the meat and she gives it to the man. Then she puts the small piece that's left in the bowl. One small piece of meat, you have to share between five! So whatever we had, we had to share it. You can't be greedy. The man is treated differently – he is the head of the family.

When I grew up things became harder. My parents forced me to marry when I was 20. They performed a marriage celebration with a man I didn't know. The man I married wasn't even in Ghana when we married – he was living in Germany. He sent someone over to come and get me.

I had two children with him, one boy and one girl. I didn't know he was a violent man when I married him. He used to beat me. He tried to beat me when I was pregnant. In 1984, my husband went back to Ghana and I stayed in Germany with the children. Then he sent me a letter and said that I had to go back to Ghana urgently. I decided to go because of the

>

"When you don't have your family, it is very hard. Family is the most important thing. They are with you so that you can make a life together."

children. But when we got to Ghana, my husband had no house, not even a room. We had to stay with his friends and sleep on the floor. We found it hard to get food to eat. It was so sad for me and my children.

One day my husband rose up against me and attacked me saying he wanted to kill me. I don't know the reason – it was something in him. I don't know what made him do these things. I ran away from him. I ran for my life. I had to leave my children.

I found a friend to live with, but it wasn't easy. I needed money to eat. I started selling children's clothes, using the money to look after myself. For years I didn't see my children. I didn't know where they were. One day I was in the market and I met my friend who told me she'd seen my children living with my sisters. When I got there, my oldest sister and her friends were all there and I said to them: "I want to take my

children." But she said if I didn't leave they would kill me. Then it came to me that if I didn't leave my country I would be killed. So again I had to run for my life.

A man who had been helping me lent me some money to buy a plane ticket and I came to the UK in 2000. I was scared. I didn't know that I could seek asylum. In 2002, I went to a solicitor and he took my statement and my passport and he said that he would send them to the Home Office. Whenever I asked him about my case, he told me that the Home Office had not sent anything yet. This went on for six years and he just kept telling me lies. When I eventually went to a new lawyer, I found out the first solicitor hadn't done anything.

All that time I was living with my friend. The church and the people there had been supporting me. My new lawyer didn't send my documents to the Home Office either until 2012. Finally, I was told I could seek asylum and was called in for an interview. The Red Cross told me I should apply for NASS (National Asylum Support Service) support, which gives you about £37 a week, and NASS accommodation.

They said they'd got a place for me in Bristol, then they changed their mind and took me to Cardiff. I stayed there for two weeks in temporary accommodation. After two weeks they moved me to Plymouth.

In Plymouth, I lived in a house with four other people. It was an old house and we were all from different cultures, mixed together. It was very difficult. Some people would eat and leave the dishes for the next day to clean. Sometimes the carpet was so dirty. The situation was so stressful – this kind of thing affects your mental health and your blood pressure. But I survived.

I was there for two years and still they refused my claim. They sent a letter telling me to go to court to appeal. I shared all my evidence, but still the Home Office didn't believe it. They try to prove what you're saying is not true. It makes your depression worse.

In the end my case was successful and I was granted refugee status. But NASS only let you stay another 28 days in your accommodation once you have status, then you have to find a new place to live. I didn't have any friends or family in Plymouth so I came back to London.

My daughter came to the UK when she was an adult. I call her and see her once in a while. My son – I don't know where he is, because of what happened.

Sometimes the Home Office think that where we come from we have a good life, so we don't need protection. But it's not true.

Kontomire with Ampesie
Mary – Ghana

Ingredients

1 small yam (or half a large yam)
3 green plantains
1 onion, peeled
4 large fresh tomatoes
1 large bunch of mixed greens
(chard, kale or spinach)
1tbsp sunflower oil
1tbsp ground turmeric

1tbsp curry powder
1tsp chilli powder, or to taste
Black pepper, to taste
1tbsp tomato puree
4 tins of sardines in oil

Serves 4 to 6

Method

Top and tail the yam, then cut into quarters lengthwise and peel. Cut into slices as thick as your thumb.

Top and tail the plantains, then peel. Scrape the plantain flesh along its length with a small sharp knife to remove the pith.

Wash the plantain and yam in cold water. Then boil together for 20 minutes. Drain.

Finely chop the onion. Coarsely chop the tomatoes.

Strip the leaves from the greens and discard the stalks. Wash the leaves then place in a pan, cover with water and blanch for 5 minutes. When cooked, drain and mash the greens in a large pestle and mortar.

Meanwhile, in a frying pan, heat the oil. Add the onions and fry gently for 5 to 10 minutes, without colouring. Then add the turmeric, curry powder, chilli powder and pepper and cook for a minute, before adding the tomatoes and tomato puree and cooking for 5 more minutes.

Add the mashed greens to the pan and turn the heat to low, adding a little water. Drain most of the oil from the sardines and add to the sauce with a little bit of the sardine oil. Cook until the sardines have warmed through.

Pile the yam and plantain onto a large serving plate, placing the fish and greens alongside.

This is a popular dish in Ghana – it's an everyday dish. It's very healthy because of the greens and the oily fish. It doesn't make you fat. I eat this dish every week.

Everyone should eat together from the main plate, using their hands. You use the yam and plantain to scoop up the fish and the greens.

Fufu with Peanut Soup
Mary – Ghana

Ingredients

2 onions, peeled

3 large tomatoes or 1 tin plum tomatoes

A thumb-sized piece of ginger, peeled

200g peanuts or peanut butter

500g goat meat (or lamb)

2 red chillies

Salt, to taste

1 whole dried fish (such as mackerel or tilapia)

For the fufu

3 green plantain, peeled

3 medium cassava, peeled

Method

Finely dice the onion. Grate the tomatoes, if using fresh. Grate the ginger.

Put one onion and the peanuts or peanut butter in a blender. If using peanuts, add a little bit of water to make it easier to blend.

Put the goat in a pan with the other onion and the tomatoes, ginger and red chillies. Add salt to taste. Add 250ml water and cook slowly for 3 hours, adding more water if necessary. Or cook for one hour in a pressure cooker. (If using lamb, reduce the cooking time to 2 hours, or 40 minutes in a pressure cooker.)

Add 500ml more water and bring the soup to the boil. Add the peanut and onion paste and cook for another 20 minutes. Break the dried fish into pieces, add to the soup and cook for a further 10 minutes. Taste and adjust seasoning.

To make the fufu:

Slice the plantain and chop the cassava. Add to a pan with boiling water and cook for 30 minutes until soft. Drain.

Using the asanka and tapoli, pound the plantain until it is soft and has formed a smooth dough. Remove. Repeat with the cassava until it has also formed a smooth dough. Add the plantain to the cassava and pound until well mixed.

Serve the fufu in a handmade clay bowl. Pour the peanut soup on top with the meat and the fish.

If you don't have an asanka and tapoli you can buy instant fufu in an African grocers. Make according to packet instructions.

My mum Comfort used to cook this dish and the whole family, including the children, would help with the cooking. We ate it every day as a family and would eat together from a big bowl in the middle. My mother and father would have a separate bowl, because they were the elders. There was no fighting, otherwise you wouldn't be allowed food. We would all sit on small stools outside and use our hands to eat. You have to pinch a bit of fufu and use it to scoop up the soup.

To make fufu properly you need to use a very large pestle and mortar (called an asanka and tapoli). And you need two people. One person pounds slowly and the other uses their hands to mix. The plantain contains iron, protein, calcium and starch. It fills you up and gives you energy and makes you sleep well. It feels healthy.

Okra Soup with Banku
Susana – Ghana

Ingredients

500g okra

2 onions, peeled

3 large tomatoes

2 hot chillies (scotch bonnet or similar)

250g beef

250g firm fish (such as salmon or mackerel)

2tbsp of vegetable or palm oil

Salt, to taste

1 smoked mackerel fillet

1 chicken stock cube

For the banku:

450g cassava dough

900g corn dough

Salt, to taste

Serves 4 to 6

Method

Top and tail the okra, cut into quarters lengthwise and finely slice. Chop the onions, tomatoes and chilli. Wash the meat and fresh fish, then cut into large pieces.

Put the oil in a large pot and heat. Add the meat and fresh fish and season with salt. Add one of the chopped onions. Cook for about 10 minutes.

Blend the second onion with the tomatoes and chillies into a paste. Add to the pot and and cook for a further 30 minutes.

Meanwhile, in a separate pan, cook the okra in boiling water for 10 minutes, stirring from time to time. Drain.

Break the smoked fish into chunks and add to the pan with the meat with 500ml hot water. Cook for 5 minutes more. Then add the okra to the pan and, after 5 minutes, add the stock cube and reduce the heat. Cook, stirring occasionally, until the okra soup is gelatinous.

While the soup is cooking, make the banku:
Mix the cassava and corn dough together with about 750ml of water, using a wooden spoon or ladle. Keep stirring and when it is forming into a ball add salt and more hot water. Place on a low heat.

Cover the dough and cook for 10 minutes. Firmly turn over the dough with the spoon, add more water and cook for 10 minutes more. Then stir until all the water is gone and the aroma rises.

Form the banku into large balls and serve alongside the okra soup.

Okra soup is very popular in Ghana. You can use a variety of meat or fish for this dish.

Banku is made from corn dough and cassava dough, which have been fermented and milled to form a rough powder that is then mixed with water. Banku is usually made using a special long-handled wooden ladle.

You should use your hands to eat this dish, tearing off pieces of banku and using it to scoop up the soup. You need to twist your wrist as you do, to break off the stretchy strings from the okra.

Maurice – Biafra

I was born in Akuma in what is now Nigeria. My dad was in the British army and my mum was studying to be a teacher. She left me when I was two and a half and my brother six months old, and came to England to do a one-year course. But unfortunately, in 1966, the Biafra war started. We lived with my paternal grandma. In our town there were only mud huts and we all had little fox holes we dug ourselves. When the bombs started you would run out of your house and run into the hole and stay there until it went quiet.

My whole day was about trying to catch lizards with my catapult. I caught rats and killed quite a few snakes – they're very tasty snakes, when you're hungry. Then a local teacher told the Red Cross we were orphans, even though our parents were in England, and the Red Cross decided to give us one meal a day. Without the Red Cross we would have died. The food they gave us was basically cornmeal mixed with powdered milk and water, but to me nothing has ever tasted as beautiful. It was survival.

Quite a lot of children I used to play with died and the main problem was food. I think that's why food means so much to me. When I was back home, we had no food, but my grandma loved us. I didn't know what it was like not to be loved. Love is better than material things.

There was a refugee programme to send children to Gabon. But when they were lining us up to go, my grandmother said: "Their parents are in England, I'm taking them home and they're not going." My biggest ambition was to go to school and they said we could go, so I couldn't understand why my grandmother, who couldn't afford to send me to school, was objecting to me going. I was very angry. But as an adult I've learnt that out of 250,000 children who went to Gabon, only 5,000 returned.

One day, I was in the bush looking after a pig and some guy in a suit came. I was always in trouble, because I was always stealing food and getting caught. And he said: "Are you Maurice Nwokeji?" He said: "Don't run. I've been sent by your father. You're going to England." I was nine and I came with my brother who was seven. But me and my brother missed our grandma, because she really was our parent. When we came here and met our parents, they were strange people to us. We didn't even know we had a little brother.

I now realise the impact it must have had on my parents, from having no children to suddenly having three – one a baby and two very traumatised war children. I take my hat off to Mum, how she must have felt as a woman watching that every day on the telly, not being able to contact us, not knowing if we were alive.

I used to feel ashamed that I was born in a mud hut. So I didn't go there, I didn't open it at all. But as I got older, I realised the damage it was doing to me and to those around me. I've come to this realisation that everyone has an intrinsic worth. It's not for you to judge what that worth is, but it's nice to realise that we all have worth and we all have something to contribute, something to say.

At the age of 39 I decided to be a musician and a Rasta man and I wrote a song which became a gateway. It took me months to write it. It was about my maternal grandmother

>

who died of hunger during the war. My mind had totally obliterated that memory. There's something that happens and your mind just shuts it down in order to survive. But this song – I never sing it in concerts or anything – every line I wrote I cried for two weeks. I couldn't record it and in the end they recorded it with me actually crying.

From that album, I got to play at the Queen Elizabeth Hall in London where I met Ethnie Nightingale, who approached me about making a film about my life. When she asked me, one of the things I realised was that there are so many people like me. I thought I was unique, but there are so many children like me. I felt that by telling my story I gave permission for others to tell their stories. When I go to schools to talk, I can see that recognition in the eyes of some of the children.

We have to change the narrative about asylum seekers and refugees. They're not people who come from a country called 'Immigratia'. They're all individual people with individual stories. And it's important that people talk, because these stories need to be told. People need to tell their stories, they need that space. Since I've talked about it, the pain is more like an ache somewhere instead of a pain right at the forefront.

Nobody wants to leave their country. I didn't come here because I wanted to come here and I didn't feel good when I was here. Not because this is not a nice country – it's a lovely country. But this is not my home. When I left, I left lots of people. Nobody wants to come here. It's cold!

Ugwumpiti, Ethnie Nightingale's film about Maurice's life, can be seen at: childmigrantstories.com/ugwumpiti/

Ofe Egusi with Eba
Maurice – Biafra

Ingredients

1kg chicken thighs or drumsticks

1tbsp ground coriander

1tbsp paprika

1tbsp vegetable oil

Salt, to taste

1 bunch of spinach or bitter leaves

50g mushrooms

1 chicken stock cube

2tbsp palm oil

200g egusi flour

500g gari

Serves 6

Method

Mix the chicken with the ground coriander, paprika, vegetable oil and a pinch of salt and put in the fridge for half an hour. Preheat the oven to 180°C/160°Fan/Gas 4. Place the chicken in a roasting tray and cook in the oven for 40 minutes.

If using bitter leaves, wash them 20 or 30 times to remove the bitterness. If using spinach, wash throughly. Slice the mushrooms.

Dissolve the chicken stock cube in 1.25 litres of boiling water and add to a large pot. Add the bitter leaves (if using), the mushrooms and palm oil and boil gently for 5 to 10 minutes.

Add the egusi flour gradually, then stir. Simmer for 10 minutes, then introduce the chicken into the pot.

Add the spinach now, if using, and simmer for 5 minutes more.

To make the eba:
Pour 1 litre of boiling water into a bowl. Gradually add the gari. Pour off any excess water and stir the gari with a wooden spatula. Add more water and stir, until it comes together to form a firm dough.

To eat, form small balls with the eba and use it to scoop up the soup.

Egusi is the most popular soup in West Africa and is eaten every day. Everyone knows how to cook it. It's extremely good for you – egusi is made from melon seeds so it's concentrated nutrients. Then you've got protein from the meat and green vegetables – it's a balanced meal.

This is my version of the recipe. I'm not sure it's traditional. My children love it. If they're refusing to eat, I make them this and they eat it happily. There is a trick to eating the eba – you use it to scoop up the soup and then you swallow the ball and leave the soup in your mouth. The eba fills your belly, but it's the soup you taste.

When we had enough money my paternal grandmother would cook egusi soup. But there was another soup we ate, made with cold water and peppercorns, which you only made if you were really poor. Nobody makes it anymore and my grandmother is gone now, but sometimes I wake up and long for it still.

My grandmother farmed until she was 90 and lived to 101. She built her own house and every year she would give us yam and cassava from her farm.

Cassava Leaf Stew
Mohamed Alie – Sierra Leone

Ingredients

1 tin black-eyed beans, or 4 handfuls
of dried black-eyed beans (optional)
500g chicken legs, skin removed
2 or 3 firm fresh fish (such as bonga
or herring)
1 onion, peeled
600ml palm oil or vegetable oil

250g smooth peanut butter
1 scotch bonnet or other hot pepper
1 whole dried fish (optional)
2 packets frozen cassava leaves, defrosted
Salt, to taste
1 chicken stock cube

Method

If using dried beans, soak overnight in cold water. Drain. Fast boil the
beans for 10 minutes until partly cooked.

Cut the chicken and fish into large chunks. Chop the onion.

Put a large pot on the heat with about 3 litres of water. Add the onion to
the pot with the oil, peanut butter, hot pepper and the dried fish, if using,
and partly cooked beans (if using dried beans).

Once the stew is boiling, add the cassava leaves to the pot. Cook for
about 20 minutes.

Add the stock cube, chicken and fresh fish. If using tinned beans, add
them now. Cook for 30 minutes more. You want the cassava leaves to
turn from bright green to dark green.

Serve with plain boiled rice.

*This is a staple meal back home –
we would cook it everyday. Here I
cook it often in large amounts and
freeze it. I like it because it is our
main food and at home we would
eat it together as a family.*

On stories

This book of rich stories and sumptuous recipes has been produced against a backdrop of hostility and an official absence of compassion towards refugees and asylum seekers across the UK and beyond. Those arriving in the UK in search of a better life are often required to tell their story in the intimidating context of an asylum or visa interview. In such spaces, their words can become burdened by the weight of potentially determining either a ticket to stay or being forced to leave. Across media and political discourses, people leaving their homes in search of something safer or better are widely depicted as intruders or objects of pity.

We compile this book in an environment in which stories about refugees and migrants prevail. Such stories can perform the function of labelling a perceived Other, of separating a mythical 'us' from an imagined 'them'. Individual stories of trauma and resilience can be used to separate the 'good' refugee from the 'bad' refugee, the deserving from the underserving. Whilst on the other hand, collective stories describing the movement of people across borders are presented through metaphors such as 'floods', 'swarms', or 'waves'. Stories used in this way can de-humanize. Those seeking a new life come to represent either a threat or a martyr – yet seldom a human being. Within this climate, stories can be used to highlight difference.

At Stories & Supper, we think that stories do matter. But they matter if the teller can have control over their own story and can tell it on their own terms. We believe that the telling and sharing of stories can contribute to an alternative narrative about migration, one that can challenge stereotypes and dispel some of the myths.

The stories that you are reading here have not been produced through a single interview with a particular purpose. They have been collected over the course of several months – or years in some cases – and through several encounters and conversations. These have included Wednesday evening meet-ups in which we have shared stories and memories of favourite meals, exchanged techniques for chopping tomatoes and pickling aubergines, or learnt how to use chopsticks or fold Chinese dumplings.

We have also held regular Saturday morning workshops, where we have created stories using drama, objects, puppets, drawing, prose and poetry. Sometimes these have been led by professional storytellers or theatre makers – including our friends at Phosphoros, Jumana Moon and Sue Mayo - or by people on our team. Rather than deepening distance and creating boundaries, we use stories as a way to find points of connection and commonality despite often having

> *"The telling and sharing of stories can contribute to an alternative narrative about migration, one that can challenge stereotypes and dispel some of the myths."*

vastly different life experiences. We have shared stories of childhood games, of childhood stories, of home cooking, and we have imagined together what superpower we would like to have and how we would use it.

There has been space to delve into memory boxes to remember, imagine and share stories of distant homes, families and places. But there has also been space to keep the box's lid firmly shut, space to not re-visit a painful past, to not share. We have journeyed into our imaginations to create alternative stories.

We hope that the stories shared in this book capture the tellers' plural identities that go far beyond their 'refugee-ness'. Stories of multiple 'I's, stories that reflect the messy patchwork of experiences that make up individual lives, but stories that also defy categorisation and resist the dehumanising narratives about refugees that pervade mainstream media and political discourse.

As well as the telling of stories, Stories & Supper takes seriously the importance of listening. As Maurice (see page 90 for his story) remarked during one of our workshops: "It's not just about speaking, it's about being heard."

These stories have also been shared, told and retold to different audiences – including the readers of this book. We hope that this process of sharing stories – told by the people who have made the journeys, who have experienced the injustices of the UK's asylum regime, who have arrived in search of something better – will contribute to a more just and humane migration narrative. This book is part of our commitment to this alternative story about migration. It is a small act of welcome. And this book is part of a collective resistance to the silencing of refugee voices.

Olivia Sheringham

Cantonese Steamed Fish
Tim Cheung – Hong Kong

Ingredients

1 shallot, peeled

2 spring onions

3tbsp vegetable or sunflower oil

50ml water

50ml light soy sauce

1tsp oyster sauce

1tsp white sugar

600g to 1kg sea bream, gutted (if smaller reduce amount of other ingredients)

Parsley to garnish (optional)

Serves about 3

Method

Roughly chop the shallots. Trim the spring onions and chop the white part, keeping the green parts until later.

Put 1tbsp oil in a pan on a low-medium heat, add the shallots and spring onion, cook until aromatic or a little bit brown, for about 2 minutes.

Add the water, soy sauce, oyster sauce and sugar. Increase the heat until boiling, for about 1 minute, then take off heat. Strain, removing the onions and saving the liquid.

Place the fish in a heatproof dish and steam in a wok or steamer for 20 to 30 minutes for a 600g to 700g fish, longer for a larger fish. You can check it's done at the thickest part on the back of the fish with a knife – the flesh should be falling off the bone. Tip away the water.

Pour the soy sauce mix around the fish but not on top of it.

Slice the green part of the spring onion into 6cm lengths, halve along the length of the strip and wash. It should curl a little. Place on top of the fish.

Heat the remaining oil over a high heat in a small saucepan until it is very hot. Immediately pour on top of the fish and spring onions. It will sizzle and run down the fish and bring out the flavours of the spring onions.

Garnish with parsley if you wish. Serve immediately while it's hot with a bowl of white rice. Share.

From when I was very small, maybe four years old, I knew how to take the bones out of fish that were cooked whole. I grew up on Kut-O island, a fishing village where there was not much meat to eat. Around the time I was 10, once I had learnt to swim, my mum let me fish on my own or with friends. Not with a stick or rod, but a fishing line with a hook. For bait we dug up earthworms, or used hermit crabs, breaking the shells first. Because we were poor, bringing fish home meant we could contribute to the family meal.

Once a month, my mum would go to the beach when it was low tide to dig for clams. She would get me to chop grass to make the fire. We ate fish almost every day. This recipe is a little more sophisticated – back then we used to cook very simply with just oil and salt, as there were very few ingredients available.

I didn't get to eat so much fish when I moved to England as a teenager. And then we ran a family takeaway business from 1970 for 33 years. But now I'm retired I cook and eat fish every day. I love all kinds of fish – herring, sprat, big or small – you can cook it in so many ways. It's really healthy and reminds me of those times fishing in Kut-O.

Theatre of Resistance

Stories & Supper have been collaborating with Phosphoros Theatre for nearly two years. Members of the company have run a number of workshops for us, helping the refugees in our team to improve their performance and storytelling skills. Their actors have also spoken at several of our supper clubs and other events.

In Autumn 2019, Phosphoros performed their show *Pizza Shop Heroes* at our 'street food and stories' event at Canon Frome Court in Ledbury, Herefordshire – incorporating Shahnaz and Abdullah from Stories & Supper into the play. It was a really special moment for us, bringing our companies together in this way. We love working with Phosphoros, as we share a commitment to providing platforms for refugees to tell their own stories, as an act of resistance.

Kate

Phosphoros Theatre is a political theatre company that makes shows with actors who came to the UK as unaccompanied child refugees. A big part of our work sees us touring around the UK going to different theatres to perform. We often have to stay the night in hotels, spend long days travelling or go and stay with my parents in Derbyshire (they're part of the company too). So, alongside learning our lines and preparing for our show, food is a very important part of Phosphoros Theatre's daily life!

Our actors come from different countries, including Afghanistan, Eritrea, Albania and Somalia. The food in these countries has some similarities, as well as big differences in how much chilli each person likes, which means it can be difficult to settle on a dish that everyone will enjoy. Aside from heat levels, we often have 15 or more people around the table so have to find meals that are quick and easy to cook but still delicious. Sometimes we get rid of the table completely and eat together on a big rug on the floor. For Phosphoros, food is family time, and we always make room for it.
Shepherd's Pie, page 108

Syed

I came to the UK in 2013 to seek asylum, because the situation back home was very dangerous for me. I came as an unaccompanied minor, which meant I was without my family. Since I was a child, I went into foster care and now I live on my own. The women in Afghanistan are generally in charge of cooking, so I suddenly had to learn how to cook when I came here. I would eat Afghan food in restaurants and it would remind me of home, and I wished I could make it.

I started asking friends and my family back home how to make my favourite dishes and slowly I learnt. Now I make food from Afghanistan a lot, both for my Afghan friends and my English friends who have never tried it. My cooking skills don't extend far beyond Afghan food quite yet, although my mates say I've become very English since I bought a cheese toastie maker!
Buranee Kadoo, page 104

Goitom

I am very good at cooking, because I learnt from my mother. For people like me who came from Eritrea as kids without their parents, it is hard to know how to make Eritrean dishes like doro wot properly. I remember when I first made it for my friends in London they were joking with me, saying there must be a girl in the kitchen secretly making it because it was so delicious! They couldn't believe I could make this special dish myself.

Like other Eritrean food, we serve doro wot on top of our traditional bread, injera. Injera is made out of teff flour and is kind of like a spongey pancake. We put the injera on a very big plate, then the food in the middle, and then we roll up slices of injera to place on top in case people want more. I really like eating in this way, because everyone sits together and we feed each other too. This is really special for us if we have guests in the house.
Doro Wot, page 106

www.phosphorostheatre.com

Buranee Kadoo
Syed Haleem Najibi – Afghanistan

Ingredients

1 butternut squash

5tbsp vegetable oil

5 cloves of garlic, peeled

1 chunk of fresh ginger, peeled (about 2tbsp when chopped)

4 big tomatoes (nice juicy ones from the market, not flavourless salad tomatoes)

1 to 5 thin fresh chillies (it depends how spicy you like it – I put in 4 or 5)

1tsp ground turmeric

2tsp ground coriander

Salt, to taste

To serve

1 bunch fresh mint

500g of natural yoghurt (to make it vegan, you can use coconut yoghurt)

1 large handful of fresh coriander

Afghan naan (or pitta)

Salad

Serves 4 as a main meal or 6-8 as a side dish

Method

Peel the butternut squash and remove the seeds. Cut into cubes about 3cm big.

Heat the oil in a big pot. You can use a large frying pan but a pot is better. Put the squash into the oil on a medium heat and cover with a lid.

Whilst the squash is softening, finely chop the garlic and ginger and add to the pot, putting the lid back on.

Next, cut the tomatoes into small pieces, along with the chillies. If you don't want too much heat, don't include the seeds of the chillies.

When the squash is quite soft, add the tomatoes and stir. Then add the spices, chillies and salt to taste. Put the lid back on to help it cook. This should take about 45 minutes. You'll know when it is ready because the liquid from the tomatoes will have disappeared.

While it is cooking, you need to prepare the serving dish.

Chop the mint very finely, then mix with the yoghurt. If you want, you can add a bit of salt too. Spread the minty yoghurt onto a large serving platter so it covers it completely.

When the squash is cooked, leave it to cool slightly. When it is still warm, spoon it onto the yoghurt, leaving a bit of yoghurt showing at the edge. Chop the fresh coriander and scatter on top. Serve with bread and salad.

I love buranee kadoo. Funnily enough though, I never actually ate it in Afghanistan.

A very popular dish back home is buranee banjan, which is exactly the same but with banjan (aubergine). We have buranee banjan as a side dish with our famous national dish kabuli pilau, which is an enormous mound of rice with slivers of carrot, raisins and pistachios, and a leg of lamb. We also serve kabuli pilau with salad, lamb kofta, mantu (steamed dumplings with spiced minced lamb) and other delicious vegetable dishes. Our mothers and sisters would make this kind of food for weddings or family gatherings. As any Afghan will tell you, hospitality is a crucial part of our culture and we are very proud of our food and looking after our guests.

I first tried buranee kadoo in a restaurant in Kilburn and really loved it. Kadoo actually means pumpkin, which is very common in Afghanistan, but in England it's easier to find butternut squash. I'd usually serve this dish with fresh naan and a salad with mango or pomegranate in it, or as an accompaniment to other dishes.

Doro Wot
Goitom – Eritrea

Ingredients

5 small onions, peeled

5 cloves of garlic, peeled

1 medium sized piece of ginger, peeled (about 3tbsp)

1 whole chicken (or, if it's easier, 12 chicken pieces – a mixture of thighs and drumsticks)

4tbsp sunflower or vegetable oil

2 large tomatoes

1tsp ground cardamom

3tbsp berbere (Ethiopian spice mix)

12 free-range eggs

Salt and pepper

Serves 6

Method

First, chop the onions very small and then put them in the pot ready for cooking. Chop the garlic and ginger.

Next, cut the chicken into 12 pieces. This step is very important, because the pieces symbolise the Twelve Apostles. This takes quite a bit of time, so don't start cooking the onions until it's done, otherwise they will burn.

When the chicken has been cut up, put the oil in the pot with the onions and put on a low heat. Add the garlic and ginger and cook together gently for about 30 minutes.

Meanwhile, chop the tomatoes. Next, add the tomatoes, spices and salt and pepper to the pot and cook for about 15 minutes more.

Then, add about 500ml of water and all the chicken and stir. Bring to the boil, then reduce to a low heat and cook until it's ready, about 1 hour.

Meanwhile, hard boil the eggs for 10 minutes. Leave to cool, then peel.

Remove the chicken from the pan and put onto a big plate.

Cook the sauce for a bit longer, until it's delicious and thick, adding the eggs so that they absorb some flavour.

Pour the sauce over the chicken. Serve with injera.

I want to share the recipe for doro wot because it is such a respected dish in my country, Eritrea, and also in Ethiopia. There are different times that we eat doro wot. Traditionally, when it's Easter we sacrifice a chicken and we cook it in this way. At a wedding, the guests will eat beef or lamb and only the bride and groom's family can eat the delicious doro wot.

To make doro wot properly is very difficult because you have to cut the chicken into 12 pieces in a specific way, not how a butcher would do it. It has rules. Making doro wot in the UK is a bit different to making it in Eritrea, because the chicken is not so fresh here. A free-range organic chicken will be better, but it's more expensive.

Also, back home, my mother would mix the traditional spices, including chilli, garlic, ginger, korarima, rue, ajwain, nigella and fenugreek. It's easier in the UK to buy berbere spice mix from a shop.

Phosphoros Shepherd's Pie
Kate – UK

Ingredients

1 large onion, peeled
4 cloves garlic (or to taste), peeled
3 carrots
1tbsp oil
500g lamb, beef or soya mince
3tbsp tomato purée
A pinch of salt
A splash of Worcestershire sauce, balsamic vinegar or soy sauce
500ml beef or vegetable stock
2tbsp onion gravy granules (optional)

For the mashed potato topping

900g floury potatoes, peeled
1 clove garlic (optional)
Salt
85g butter
50-100ml milk
Cheddar cheese, grated

Peas to serve

Serves 4 as a main course

Method

Preheat the oven to 180°C/ Gas Mark 4

Dice the onion, crush the garlic and finely chop the carrots. Heat the oil in a large pot or frying pan and then fry the onions and garlic gently for about 10 minutes, until they're soft. Then add the carrots, frying for 5 more minutes. Add whatever mince you're using, and let it brown. If you're using vegetarian mince this won't take long.

Add the tomato purée, salt and whatever sauce you want to add some depth. Worcestershire sauce is a safe option (although not vegetarian). When everything is cooking nicely, add the stock. If you're using vegetable stock, it is wise to add some extra onion gravy granules for more flavour. Let it simmer for about 40 minutes.

Meanwhile, make the mashed potato topping: Cut the potatoes into 4cm chunks so they cook quicker. Boil until they're soft (you can test with a knife). Mash the potatoes together with some extra crushed garlic if you like, a pinch of salt, a knob of butter to taste and milk to make it smooth.

When it's finished, tip the meat or soya into a casserole dish, then carefully spoon the mashed potatoes over the top. Use the back of a spoon to smooth it down, then use a fork to make a pattern.

Bake in the oven for 20 minutes, or until the mixture is bubbling. Take it out of the oven and sprinkle some cheese on top and pop under the grill to make a nice crispy topping. Serve with a big bowl of peas and invite everyone to customise it however they want.

The first time Phosphoros visited Derbyshire, my dad Liam made Shepherd's Pie. This was the first time some of our actors had tried traditional English food. Liam is from Cumbria and Shepherd's Pie reminds him of his childhood.

Comforting food like this is the perfect way to end a long day of rehearsals, to chat about what is going on in our lives and support each other through ups and downs. Fast forward a few years and Shepherd's Pie remains one of our absolute favourite dishes and some of our actors even cook it for their friends in their own homes.

This simple recipe is only the beginning. Every meal table at Phosphoros HQ is strewn with sauce bottles, chillies, spices and pickles, ready to boost flavour and add a personal twist. Some of our favourites include tortilla wraps or pitta, green chillies and chilli flakes. Syed likes to dip garlic naan into his Shepherd's Pie. Emirjon sprinkles his with cheese. Goitom covers his in Greek yoghurt and Liam drizzles sweet chilli sauce on his. The possibilities are endless – we hope you enjoy!

Mohamed Alie – Sierra Leone

I was born in 1986 in a small town called Bumpeh in the Kono district of Sierra Leone. Kono is in the East of Sierra Leone, close to the border with Liberia, and it is famous for diamonds. Everywhere you go there are diamonds. You can see them in the ground, but you have to know how to dig for them.

I lived there with my family. My father had four wives and a total of 20 children. When I was born, he was living with two wives, and I was the first of 10 children he had with my mother, his fourth wife. He had already had 10 children, so when I was born we were 11 children in the house. It was a busy household! All the boys slept in one room and the girls in another. The house was small, but there was a big shop at the front that sold provisions – milk, sugar, rice. My father was a businessman. As well as the shop, he owned several petrol stations and was a diamond dealer. He had a lot of cars and everyone in the town knew him.

My family were very strict Muslims. We would pray five times a day. My older siblings could recite the whole of the Qur'an. My father is Fula, one of the main ethnic groups in Sierra Leone. His first wife is Fula and my mother is Susu. At home they would speak Fula, but I didn't really know how to speak it. I don't know my language. I was taught to speak Krio – a kind of pidgin English that's a mix of many languages. A lot of words are similar to English. To say "come on" you say "cam".

I don't remember too much about my early childhood, though my mother has told me about the beautiful landscapes. I do remember the meals we used to eat together. In the mornings we would eat bread with fresh stew made with meat or fish. And we would all drink tea. Sometimes, even for breakfast we would cook rice, with okra, jakato (a kind of squash) and sardines. When my father was looking I would eat with my right hand (we are Muslim so we have to eat with our right hand). But when he wasn't there I would always eat with my left hand. I'm naturally left-handed so this was much easier! For lunch we would eat heavy rice, a lot of meat cooked with cassava leaves or potato leaves. I loved cooking, I would sometimes cook with my mum. I loved cooking cassava leaves, especially with black-eyed beans and okra.

When I was five, I started going to the local primary school. One day I was late for school and the teacher flogged my hand. By this time, there were 14 children in our household. I remember the day that the rebels attacked. They attacked the whole of the Kono district. We woke up early for prayers and we started hearing sounds – 'kik, kik, kik' and then 'boom, boom'. My father said to my mother, "don't worry, don't worry". But we could hear thousands of people in the streets. The rebels had been looting neighbouring villages. They were coming closer. As the noise got louder, my father seemed really worried. He had 14 children, his businesses, his cars – a lot to lose. He locked us all in the house and we hid in a room at the back. We stayed quiet.

The loud noises were coming from 10 miles away, but we knew the rebels were coming to our town. We knew that when they came they would take everything. In the end my father decided that we should leave. He said we should leave out of the back door (a door we never used) so we could escape and not be seen. But as soon as we got outside the door, we saw the rebels in front of us. They stopped us. They all had guns. My mother held my hand, she was crying. One of the rebels said that if she didn't give me to them they would kill her. So they took me away.

They took me to the forest. I didn't know what happened to my family. I didn't see them for 10 years. I found out later that they also captured two of my sisters.

I walked miles with the rebels. I can still feel pain now because I had to carry so much. We would walk miles across the country and steal from all the villages. I also had to carry food, ammunition. If they thought you were lazy they would beat you, they would kick you. They would force you to take drugs to make you more active. Nobody was kind. They wanted to kill people. They wanted to steal things. They were cruel.

As we travelled, the rebels also captured other children. I didn't have friends. All I could think about was when I was going to see my parents. I don't remember playing with the other kids. I just remember fatigue, having to cook for them, having to do everything for them. We walked a thousand miles in total.

The only time I felt happy was when we arrived in Makeni, in the Northern part of Sierra Leone. By that time, things had started to calm down. The peace talks had started, and there were commanders who were controlling things a bit more. They didn't allow the rebels to beat us.

I was 16 when we arrived in Makeni, 10 years after I had been captured. I remember the day that a commander came and took us to the park, where there were people from the UN. They took my name, gave me my registration number and told me to stand in line. They gave us food and water and told us to wait. I was taken in a car and we travelled to the west of the country, to Waterloo, a rural part of the country very close to the capital, Freetown. We stopped there and they showed me where to sleep.

UNICEF had set up a camp there and we were given counselling. I lived on that camp for four years. I still hadn't heard about my family. I don't know if they heard something announced on the radio, but eventually they came looking for me. I found out later that my sisters were there too, but I didn't know. The camp was huge, the size of a small town, with lots of different places to live.

I was 20 when my parents came to find me. I was happy to see them, but it was also very strange. I didn't recognise them. It took me a while to realise it was my mother. It was hard to be reunited after such a long time. By that time, my parents had moved to Freetown. I went back to live with them and my parents found a private school for me to go to. They wanted to help me, but I found it difficult to cope being in a class with children who were much younger than me.

After the rebel war, everyone was very suspicious and angry. It was very hard to adapt. I had been with the rebels for 10 years. I was very sensitive. I found it hard to be with other children. I was determined to carry on studying and took some private classes. After two

"After the rebel war, everyone was very suspicious and angry. It was very hard to adapt."

years, I was able to pass my West African Senior School Certificate Examination. I went to college and completed a diploma in Early Childhood Education at the University of Sierra Leone. I passed the exam in two years and began a degree in Sociology. I finished the second year of the course, but then unfortunately experienced another traumatic event, which led to me leaving Sierra Leone.

I arrived in London in October 2017. I came to see my sister, who was living in London and invited me for her graduation. But she rejected me because of my sexuality and I could not continue living with her. Things have been tough. I am still waiting for the outcome of my asylum claim.

I haven't travelled much in the UK, but I like it here in London. I like the people, I like the structures, I like the system here. You have freedom here. I now have a scholarship to study a foundation course in Applied Psychology at Birkbeck University, which I have just started. I am very happy to be studying again. And I'm happy to be able to tell my story.

ENDINGS

Czech Fruit Cake
Eva & Karel – Czech Republic

Ingredients

For the dough:

30g of fresh yeast (or 15g active dry yeast, or 12g instant yeast)

500g of polohruba flour (or 250g of plain flour and 250g of fine semolina)

80g of granulated sugar

300ml of milk

70g of unsalted butter

2 free-range egg yolks

500g fresh plums, apricots, peaches or nectarines

For the crumble:

110g plain flour

30g caster sugar

70g cold, unsalted butter

Method

Preheat the oven to 180°C/160°Fan/Gas 4. Grease and line a deep baking tray, about 30cm x 20cm, or you can use one big and one small round cake tin.

If using fresh yeast, crumble into a small bowl and add a teaspoon of sugar and a little lukewarm water or milk then mash with a fork to dissolve. Leave for five minutes, until it starts to foam. If using dry yeast, add to a little lukewarm water with a pinch of sugar to rehydrate.

To make the dough: Mix the flour and sugar in a mixing bowl, adding the instant yeast now, if using.

Heat the milk – it needs to be just warm enough to melt the butter. Switch off the heat and then add the butter. When the butter has melted, whisk in the egg yolks. Add the milk mixture and the reconstituted yeast (if using) into the dry ingredients. Mix together to make a smooth dough.

Leave the dough to rise in a warm place, covered by a tea towel, for about an hour, or until it doubles in size.

Meanwhile, make the crumble: Mix the flour and sugar. Cut the butter into small cubes and rub into the flour until it forms large crumbs.

Remove stones from the fruit and halve or slice, depending on the size.

After the dough has risen, spread it into the baking tray and leave to rise again for 30 minutes. Then put a layer of the fruit on the dough and cover it with crumble. Bake for 30 minutes or longer, until the dough is fully baked and the fruit is soft.

Karel and Eva (pictured)

At the beginning I have to explain the following: In the UK we have either plain or self-raising wheat flour. Czechs have three types of wheat flour – plain, semi coarse (polohruba in Czech) and coarse flour (hruba in Czech). For this cake you need to use semi-coarse (polohruba) flour. This type of flour is quite difficult to buy in the UK, but you can mix plain flour and semolina to get the right mixture of flour.

For fruit toppings you can use plums (Victoria or President), apricots, peaches or nectarines.

To make the dough rise, it is traditional to put it into your bed, under the duvet. You don't have to be in bed at the time.

Grandma Leah's Yeast Cake
Inbar – Israel

Ingredients

425g bread flour (plus extra for kneading)

30g fresh yeast (or 15g dry yeast,

or 12g of fast action yest)

125ml lukewarm water

150 to 200g granulated sugar

150g unsalted butter, softened

1 free-range egg

3tbsp cocoa

Glaze (optional)

2tbsp of granulated sugar

A little water

Method

Lightly grease a bundt tin, about 20cm to 24cm diameter.

Put the flour in a large mixing bowl. Make a hole in the middle and add the yeast. Add a little of the warm water and mix with the yeast. Leave for 20 minutes until it begins to bubble. If you are using fast action yeast, you can add it to the flour with a little water and go to the next step now.

Add 50g sugar and 50g butter to the dough. Mix thoroughly. Add the remaining water and the egg, beaten lightly, and mix. If the dough is too dry, you can add a little more water. Cover the dough and leave to rise for about an hour or until doubled in size.

Roll the dough out as thinly as possible into an oblong shape and spread with the remaining butter. Mix the cocoa with the remaining sugar (reducing the sugar for a less sweet cake), and shake over the butter.

Starting at one of the long ends, roll the dough tightly like a swiss roll and then curl round in a circle in the tin, seam side up, joining the ends together. Leave to rise in the tin, covered with a tea towel, until double in size – about half an hour or more.

Meanwhile, preheat the oven to 200°C/180°C Fan/Gas 6. When the dough has risen, bake for 30 minutes, or longer, until golden and cooked.

If using the glaze, mix the sugar with the water until dissolved. Brush over the warm cake.

My mum made this cake regularly. The recipe originally came from her grandma who was her main carer when she grew up in Palestine during the Second World War. The cake is traditionally baked in a tin called a wonderpot, which my mum put in the oven, but was originally made to go on top of the stove like a Dutch oven.

Lemon Love Child
Helen – UK

Ingredients

200g fine semolina
100g ground almonds
2tsp baking powder
1 lemon
150g unsalted butter, softened
225g caster sugar
3 large free-range eggs
250ml natural Greek yoghurt

For the syrup:

2 or 3 lemons, to make 100ml of
lemon juice
150g caster sugar

Method

Preheat the oven to 180°C/160°C Fan/Gas 4. Grease and line a 24cm springform cake tin.

In a mixing bowl, mix the dry ingredients together evenly, sifting the baking powder if necessary to remove any lumps.

Zest the lemon. Cream the butter and sugar together with the lemon zest, in a stand mixer or by hand with a wooden spoon, until light and fluffy.

Beat the eggs lightly in a small bowl.

Add the eggs gradually to the butter and sugar and beat between each addition. You can add a spoonful of the dry ingredients to stop the mixture splitting, if necessary.

Once all the eggs have been incorporated, add half the dry ingredients and beat. Then add half the yoghurt and beat to mix. Repeat adding the rest of the dry ingredients and then the rest of the yoghurt, beating after each addition.

Pour the mixture into the prepared cake tin and level it with the back of a spoon. Put into the pre-heated oven and bake for 40 minutes, or until a skewer comes out clean.

While the cake is cooking, prepare the syrup. Squeeze the lemons to get 100ml of juice and put the juice into a small pan with the caster sugar. Heat gently, stirring to dissolve the sugar. Cook on a low heat for a few minutes to thicken slightly. Cool.

As soon as the cake comes out of the oven, pour over the syrup, pausing if necessary to allow it to sink in.

We've served various versions of basbousa – a dense, syrupy semolina cake made all over the Middle East and North Africa – at several of our supper clubs. We've also eaten many, many slices of homemade cake after our weekly workshops, with lemon drizzle being the firm favourite.

This recipe is an attempt to bring the two together. A semolina cake, drenched in lemon syrup, it's the love child of basbousa and lemon drizzle. Hence the name.

Jin Dui and Lor Mai Chi
Tim Cheung – Hong Kong

Jin Dui (Sesame balls)

450g glutinous rice flour

60g wheat starch

1tsp baking powder

5tbsp granulated sugar

2tbsp vegetable oil

250ml cold water

450g red bean paste

140g sesame seeds, toasted

Method

Place the glutinous rice flour into a bowl, making a hole like a volcano. Add the wheat starch, baking powder, sugar and oil into the middle.

Slowly add the water, from the centre to the outside, with one hand, mixing slowly with the other in one direction only. Don't go back in the other direction or it will clump. Do not let the water spill out of the walls of the flour. Keep mixing until you have a soft dough. Add more water if it is too dry. If there is too much flour the jin dui will crack.

Roll the red bean paste into balls 2cm in diameter. Pour the sesame seeds onto a large plate.

Roll the dough into a sausage about 4cm thick. Divide into 24 pieces. Take one piece of dough and roll into a disc about 5cm in diameter. Place a ball of red bean paste into the middle of the disc and roll the dough around the paste, being careful not to crack the dough or let the paste come out. Roll the ball into a sphere between your palms, then roll in the sesame seeds. Repeat with the other 23.

Using a deep fat fryer, heat the oil to 160°C, or fill a pan with enough oil to deep fry. Fry balls for 10 minutes until golden brown. After 4 to 5 minutes they should float to the top and turn over. Otherwise, turn with a slotted spoon. Place on kitchen paper to soak up excess oil.

Lor Mai Chi

(Glutinous Rice Balls)

450g glutinous rice flour

60g rice flour

450ml semi-skimmed milk

250ml water

100g granulated sugar

1tbsp vegetable oil, plus extra

Filling

80g monkey nuts, shelled and skins rubbed off

30g granulated sugar

40g sesame seeds, toasted

5tbsp fine desiccated coconut

Method

Mix the rice flours. Add milk, water, oil and sugar and mix thoroughly. Transfer to a lightly-oiled flat-bottomed dish (about 20cm).

Steam for about 20 minutes, until the bottom is cooked. Leave to cool slightly.

Meanwhile for filling: crush the nuts and mix with the sugar and sesame seeds. Put the coconut in a separate bowl.

Wearing gloves covered with a small amount of oil, knead 2tbsp of the rice dough into a small disc until flat.

Cup the disc so that it forms a bowl shape in one hand and spoon in 1tbsp of the nut mixture.

Starting from one end carefully pinch dough together until the mixture is completely enclosed. Roll ball in coconut until fully covered.

Place finished balls in small paper cupcake cases.

Sago Pudding with Gula Melaka
Jane – Malaysia

Ingredients

1.5 litres of water
200g small sago pearls or seeds
250ml coconut milk
2 pandan leaves
Salt
70g palm sugar (or light brown soft sugar)
3tbsp water

Makes 4 to 6 individual puddings
(depending on size of bowls)

Method

Bring the water to the boil and add the sago. Reduce the heat and keep stirring until all the the sago has become translucent. This will take about 20 to 30 minutes.

Using a large sieve, drain the sago and wash off any starch with cold running water.

Pour into the pudding bowls and put in the fridge until set.

Using a small saucepan, heat the coconut milk, pandan leaves and salt, knotting the pandan leaves so they fit in the pan. Cook slowly on a low heat, stirring constantly until bubbling and then set aside to cool. Remove the pandan leaves.

In another small saucepan melt the sugar and 3 tablespoons of water on a low heat for approximately 5 minutes until it thickens. Cool.

Take out the chilled puddings and drizzle the coconut milk and syrup over the top.

Tuck in.

As a child in Malaya (now Malaysia) this was always a very special treat when we ate out as a family. It instantly transports me back to an idyllic childhood in the Far East as an 'Army Brat'. Gula Melaka is a sweet syrup made from palm sugar which comes from the sap of flowers from palm trees, often coconut palm. It is very sweet so only small portions are needed. All ingredients should be available from oriental supermarkets.

Kahraman – Turkey

I am a Kurd from Turkey. I came to London as a refugee on a spring day in 2001. I'll tell you a little story from my journey, as a refugee, to London.

Back in Turkey, I had a degree in International Relations. When I passed the exam to enter the politics department, my parents hoped that I was going to be an important diplomat. They were naive, of course.

At the time, a relatively more liberal government was in power in Turkey, and there were Kurdish ministers in the cabinet. But they were from privileged families, who rejected their Kurdish roots. They believed in the Turkish nationalist project and were ready to sacrifice their own identity.

This was at the time when the EU was an important project for the Turkish government, and Brussels was the symbol of international politics for us. So, the big dream in my family was for me to work in Brussels after graduation.

In my second year at university, I realised that being a diplomat in Brussels (or elsewhere) could only be a dream for me. Someone like me, who had been involved in leftist politics for years and who came from an ordinary Kurdish family, could not be a diplomat. It was a role which had an aristocratic status in the state hierarchy.

A few years after my graduation, after being arrested by the police many times and becoming well-known to the police, I had to leave the country.

The aim was to go to London where many members of my family lived. But how would I do that? We had to make a plan. My father found someone who arranged a passport for me to use to go to Europe. We had to find a network, who would organise the journey to London. We found one at a price!

When the Albanian network told me that they had arranged a safe journey for me, and a group of people from different countries, we thought this would be it. Because we paid these people. I did not know that we would end up somewhere in Europe, under a lorry where I was placed together with refugees from different countries.

Don't think that I was confused about this arrangement because of my little English, by the way. I could make sentences in simple present and simple past tense only, but I could communicate with people. My English was actually helpful when the police caught us under a lorry.

It was really ironic when I noticed that we had been taken to a police station in the suburbs of Brussels. At that moment, I remembered my parents' dream of seeing me as a diplomat in Brussels. They treated us well in the police station. At the end of the day, they were going to send us back to where we had come from.

We weren't a big trouble for them. That's why they weren't violent. It was like staying in a hotel for me, after my encounters with the Turkish police.   >

When you have to go through a journey like that, you have to see the humour in it, in order to survive. I remember a funny exchange with a young policeman at the station.

There was a picture of Jean-Claude van Damme on the wall of the station. I looked at the picture and thought about how they could put up that poster in a police station, a branch of a government institution.

The young policeman asked me if I knew who that was. I replied, "a very famous Belgian actor!" He was so pleased to hear me say that, that he offered me food.

I knew that my love for cinema would be useful one day!

They sent us back the next morning. That journey was my first visit to Brussels, not as a diplomat, but as a refugee who was trying to reach a safer country.

After trying many different routes, I finally arrived in London.

I went to Brussels a few years ago, with my British passport this time. I walked around the city, visiting the EU building as a legal citizen. While drinking with my friends, I remembered my first half-visit there. It was good to be back as a legal person!

EXTRAS

Cornbread
Sanchia – UK

Ingredients

125g melted butter, or 125ml good olive oil for a more savoury flavour

2 free-range eggs

300ml yoghurt

180ml milk

Optional: 80g light soft brown sugar or honey, or 30g molasses and 50g sugar for a darker bread

250g coarse cornmeal or polenta bramata (not instant polenta)

350g plain flour (or light spelt flour)

4tsp baking powder

1tsp sea salt

Optional: fresh corn kernels sliced from 2 cobs, or one tin of sweetcorn kernels

Variations:

Chopped red chilli, sliced spring onions and fresh coriander

Dried oregano, Aleppo flakes and crumbled feta cheese

Sliced jalapenos and cheddar

Lemon zest, fennel seeds and parmesan

Crispy smoked bacon and sage (use the bacon fat for the skillet)

Method

Preheat your oven to 200°C/180°Fan/Gas 6.

Save 2 tablespoons of the melted butter or olive oil. Whisk the rest with the two eggs, yoghurt and milk, and the honey or molasses, if using any.

Sift the cornmeal with the flour, baking powder and salt. Add the sugar to this dry mix, if you are using any.

Heat a skillet/tatin dish/oven-proof frying pan with the reserved spoon of butter or oil.

Combine the wet mix with the dry mix, add corn kernels if you like, or any other flavourings, reserving some of what you choose to sprinkle on top.

When the skillet is smoking hot, pour in the mixture and add any toppings. Put straight into the oven for 20 to 25 minutes (depending on size of pan and depth of the bread). It should be risen, golden and springy.

It is best, but not essential, if it cools a little bit before eating. If you don't eat it all in one sitting, you can fry slices in butter the next day.

Cornbread was born in Native American communities, but has travelled across continents since and been refashioned by many cultures on its way. There are yeasted ways, unleavened ways, and loaves that lift with baking powder like a soda bread. There are yoghurt versions, buttermilk versions, and some made with kefir. Some drip with butter, some carry a distinctive tang of olive oil, and some are soaked in bacon fat. It is often sweetened with honey, sugar or molasses. I first wanted to make a loaf when I was eight, and reading Little House on the Prairie, when Ma's handprint on the loaves was sweetening enough.

I make a lot of different versions of this basic recipe, depending on what it will be served with. It's great with shakshuka, Turkish eggs, labneh, chowder, chilli, Boston baked beans, tagines, any kind of stew really or, as shown on page 18, with Anchovy Birds.

Paratha
Tasnim – Bangladesh

Ingredients
250g plain flour
½tsp salt
5tbsp vegetable oil, plus extra for brushing
250ml lukewarm water

Makes about 6 to 8 paratha depending on size.

Method
Mix the flour and salt together. Make a well in the middle and add a tablespoon of oil and about half of the water.

Mix together using your hands.

Gradually add the rest of the water and mix until it forms a soft dough. You might not need to use all of it.

Divide the dough into balls of about 6cm diameter. Cover the balls with a damp tea-towel and rest for half an hour.

Lightly flour the first ball of dough and roll it out into a disc about 2mm thick. Brush the surface of the paratha with a thin layer of oil.

Starting from one edge, roll the dough tightly to form a sausage shape. Starting from one end, coil the dough tightly to form a snail shape, tucking the end into the centre of the coil. Lightly flour again, then roll the coil back into a disc of about 2mm thick.

Heat one tablespoon of oil in a chapati pan or non-stick frying pan on a medium heat. Place the paratha in the pan and cook until there are golden brown spots, flipping it to cook both sides.

Repeat for the rest of the dough.

Serve with dal, vegetable or meat curry, or whatever you wish!

My fondest memories of eating these are when my cousins would stay over and mum would make us parathas to eat in the morning, with chicken korma or a lamb curry. My cousins still talk about how much they enjoyed her food as children.

Mish – Spicy yoghurt dip
Hawari – Sudan

Ingredients
1tbsp nigella seeds
1tsp fenugreek seeds
5 cloves garlic, peeled
5 green chillies
1kg natural yogurt

Method
Toast the nigella and fenugreek seeds without browning.

Cut the garlic cloves in half. If you want to increase the heat, cut the chillies in half lengthwise, but don't remove the seeds. Otherwise leave the chillies whole for a milder heat.

Mix all the ingredients in a container that has a tight lid and leave at room temperature for at least 8 hours. It is now ready to use or can be kept in the fridge until needed.

Tamarind Chutney
Shahnaz – India

Ingredients
6-7 green chillies
1 bulb garlic
A handful of fresh coriander
100g tamarind paste (not concentrate)
1tbsp ground cumin
Salt, to taste

Method
Remove the stems from the chillies. Remove the seeds if you want a milder chutney.

Separate and peel the garlic cloves.

Wash the coriander.

Blend all the ingredients together using a food processor or stick blender.

Season with salt, to taste.

Mango Chutney (pictured on page 12)
Shahnaz – India

Ingredients
1 large sour green mango
5 green chillies
1 bulb garlic
1 small bunch coriander
1 small bunch mint
Salt, to taste

Method
Peel the mango, roughly chop the flesh and discard the stone.

Remove the stems from the chillies. Remove the seeds if you want a milder chutney.

Separate and peel the garlic cloves.

Wash the herbs

Blend all the ingredients together using a food processor or stick blender, season to taste.

Tahini dressing

Ingredients
1 clove garlic, peeled
4tbsp tahini
Juice of 1 lemon
Sea salt to taste

Method
Crush the garlic and place in a small bowl. Add the tahini and the juice of half a lemon. Mix to form a stiff paste. Add cold water gradually and mix to get the desired consistency (like double cream). Add salt. Taste and adjust with extra lemon juice or salt as desired.

Lime water
Winnie – Guyana

Ingredients

2 litres water

10-15 limes (depending on size and juiciness)

70-100g sugar

1tsp vanilla essence

Crushed ice, as desired

Makes 2 litres, enough for 8 large glasses

Method

Squeeze the juice of all the limes.

Add the juice to the water.

Stir in the sugar, vanilla essence and crushed ice.

Mix it all together and taste, adding more lime juice or sugar to suit your tastebuds.

Serve and enjoy!

We had no fizzy drinks, we used to make our own. Everything was natural. My grandma Philomena would make lime water every day. It was kept in a big jug in the corner of the room. Grandma would never put the drink on the table. She had to see that your plate was empty or you weren't allowed to have any. I remember we had to set the table. I used to hate doing it, "cos that's a girl's job". I was the only girl, with two boys. And I was naughty!

Mint Tea

WE USUALLY SERVE MINT TEA AT THE END OF OUR SUPPER CLUB MEALS – THE FRESH MINT LEAVES ARE ALWAYS A HIT

Ingredients

A handful of fresh mint leaves

Boiling water

Sugar cubes

Method

Place a few mint leaves in each tea glass. Add boiling water.

Serve with sugar cubes on the side.

Ingredients

Being based in East London, we're lucky to have access to a huge range of shops selling food from around the world. If you also live in a big city, many of the ingredients below can be found in African, Indian, Turkish or Chinese shops, for example. If not, many of the larger supermarkets now stock a lot of these ingredients. And if you can't find them there, you might find them online, or you can use one of the substitutes we have suggested.

Ajwain seeds: These seeds are used in Indian cooking and are said to aid digestion. They look similar to cumin seeds, but their flavour is more like dried thyme or caraway.

Berbere: A hot spice blend used in Ethiopian and Eritrean cuisine, which includes chilli, ginger, korarima, rue, ajwain, nigella and fenugreek. Every cook has their own version, but you can buy a pre-made blend.

Bottle gourd: Also known as kaddu, this is a light green-skinned, firm squash which features in Indian cuisine. You can use courgette as a substitute, but reduce the cooking time.

Cassava: Cassava is a starchy root vegetable or tuber, which can be cooked in a variety of ways and is used to make tapioca. It is common across Africa and South America and the root should not be eaten raw.

Cassava leaves: Used in African cuisine, fresh cassava leaves need to be washed and soaked in boiling water and pounded before use to remove naturally occurring cyanide. For ease of use they can be bought frozen and ready prepared.

Cornmeal: Ground yellow corn, which is sold in fine or coarse grain varieties. Coarse cornmeal is the same as Italian polenta. Fine cornmeal is sometimes also called cornflour, but shouldn't be confused with the white cornflour used to thicken gravy.

Dried Limes: Limes that have been salted and then dried until hard, they are used in Iranian and Kurdish cooking to add an intense citrus flavour to stews.

Egusi: These are melon seeds that can be bought as dried seeds or ground into a coarse flour. They are used in West African cuisine, especially in Nigeria.

Fufu: A staple food in West Africa. The Ghanaian method involves pounding separate portions of cassava and green plantain flour with water, before mixing them together. Instant fufu is available for those without the means for pounding.

Gari: A grain produced from processed cassava. It is mixed with water to make eba, a dough which is eaten especially in Nigeria with soups.

Glutinous rice flour: This is made from short-grain sticky rice, and is used to make various Chinese sweets and desserts.

Gram Flour: A flour made from ground chick peas or channa dal, used in pakoras, bhajis and other recipes from the Indian subcontinent.

Harina PAN Maize flour: The most common brand of pre-cooked maize flour used in Venezuela to make arepas. You can substitute another brand but you must make sure you are buying pre-cooked maize flour if you are making arepas.

Semolina: A coarse flour made from durum wheat, semolina can be used in bread, pasta and porridge. It is also used in cakes to give a coarser texture and has a more golden colour than all-purpose flour.

Kaffir lime leaves: The kaffir lime is a citrus fruit found in South East Asia. The leaves have an intense citrus aroma and are used in Vietnamese, Thai, Malaysian and Burmese cuisine.

Kırık Pirinc: Broken grains of basmati rice used in Turkish and Cypriot cuisine to add substance to soups and other dishes. If you can't find broken basmati you can use regular long grain or basmati rice but it might take a bit longer to cook.

Lotus bean paste: A Chinese dessert ingredient, this is a sweet smooth paste made from dried lotus seeds.

Palm oil: The bright red oil of the palm tree, this is used a lot in West African cuisine. Sustainable palm oil can be found, but is not widely available. Alternatives are coconut oil, rapeseed or sunflower oil, although these are not as strongly flavoured.

Palm sugar: Palm sugar has a deeper and richer flavor than refined white sugar. You can use muscovado or soft brown sugar as an alternative.

Pandan leaves: Pandan is a herbaceous, tropical plant that grows in South-East Asia, and has a sweet aroma. The long green leaves are used to flavour sweet and savoury dishes. It can be bought fresh or frozen.

Paneer: A fresh unsalted white cheese common in Indian cuisine. It holds its shape when cooked and pairs well with strong spicy flavours.

Plantain: Plantain are members of the banana family, but are starchier and lower in sugar. Green plantains can be boiled, mashed or fried and should be treated more like potato. You need to remove the pith as well as the skin. Yellow or black plantains are sweeter and can be fried in slices and served with rice dishes.

Polohruba mouka: This is a semi-coarse Czech wheat flour. If you can't find it you can use an equal mixture of plain all-purpose flour and fine semolina.

Red bean paste: Also called adzuki bean paste, this paste is used in East Asian cuisines.

Sago pearls: Rolled balls of starch made from the sago palm, sago pearls are used to make desserts. They are similar to tapioca (which is made from cassava) and become translucent when cooked. They are produced in different sizes.

Tamarind: The brown pulp from the fruit of the tamarind tree, which is used in a South-East Asian cooking, especially in Hyderabad. It can be bought as a paste or a concentrate, or in blocks with or without seeds. The blocks with seeds produce the best result but need to be soaked in water so the pulp can extracted and the seeds discarded.

Toor dal: Also known as yellow lentils or split pigeon peas, toor dal has a nutty earthy flavour and is a key ingredient in Indian dishes, especially sambar. It needs soaking before cooking.

Vine leaves: The leaves of the grape vine are used in Mediterranean and Middle Eastern cooking, usually rolled and stuffed with rice and sometimes meat. Fresh vine leaves are the best but you can also buy them preserved in vinegar. Preserved vine leaves need to be washed several times.

Wiri wiri (Guyana peppers): Small round chillies with a cherry-like appearance, also known as hot cherry or bird cherry peppers. They are almost as spicy as habanero or scotch bonnet peppers, which can be used as a substitute.

Wheat starch A white flour used to make dumplings, doughs and to thicken sauces.

Yam: A tuber common in Africa, the Caribbean and South America. The flesh can be white or yellow and can be mashed, fried or roasted. It is also used to make fufu.

Index

Index

Thanks to

Phosphoros Theatre, Jumana Moon and Sue Mayo for their ongoing support with storytelling; Ed Andrews, Amy Bedford, Lou Budd and Amelia Hart at Waltham Forest Borough of Culture; Gnome House, Hornbeam Cafe and The Bank Job (Hoe Street Central Bank); Victoria at Stow Brothers; Laura Kerry and Morag McGuire at Artillery; Wilna Fourie at The Barbican; Del Taylor; Deniz Huseyin, Zeki and Rafet Taylor; Helen Cardwell, Gemma Hughes and Rachel Tiernan for additional recipe testing. Plus, a big thank you to all the people who supported our crowdfunder so that we could produce a book worthy of its contributors: Andrew Sharp, Angel, Angela Junanto, Alison Griffin, Alison Hay, Ben Pitcher and Rebecca Bramall, Bonnie, Bridget Taylor, Cathy McLoughlin, Charlie Bigham, Claire, Dr Craig A Nelson, Daniela Cabral, David and Gill Sudbery, David Cooke, David Thompson, Deniz Emre Dag, Emma Wolf, Frances Lowndes, Hilary Powell, Jackie, Jamie Masraff, Jane Lowery, Janet ET, Jenni Regan, Jess and James, Jo Cattell, Joe Noar, Kathryn Grant, Lara Hayim, Lara Speicher, Laura, Laura Kerry, Len Dunne, Lianna Merner, Mandy Kullar, Nessa Tierney, Paul Mylrea, Pavlos Christodoulou, Perry Walker, Priscilla Sheringham, Rachel Tiernan, Ross Williams, Rowan Constantinou-Stygal, Sabine Edwards, Sarah Walker, Shabna Begum, Sheena Cameron, Tenzing, Tina Tse, Tom Mowat, Victor Figueroa, Wendy Anderson and all our anonymous supporters.

Thanks also to everyone who has ever been to one of our supper clubs, events or workshops; and everyone who spreads the word about what we do. And finally, all our love and thanks to everyone in the Stories & Supper family for being part of this adventure.

5). 菜油　　　　　　2湯匙
6). 清水　　　　　　250ml
7). 芝麻　　　　　　140g

餡料：

蓮蓉或豆沙

做法：

將1至6材料搓成粉團,然後
分成24隻小粉團,壓扁包餡
黏上芝麻,開油鑊至160度火